PYRAMID

SPIRITUAL JOURNEY COMPANION

DR. YADUVIR SINGH

Made with ♥ on the Notion Press Platform
www.notionpress.com

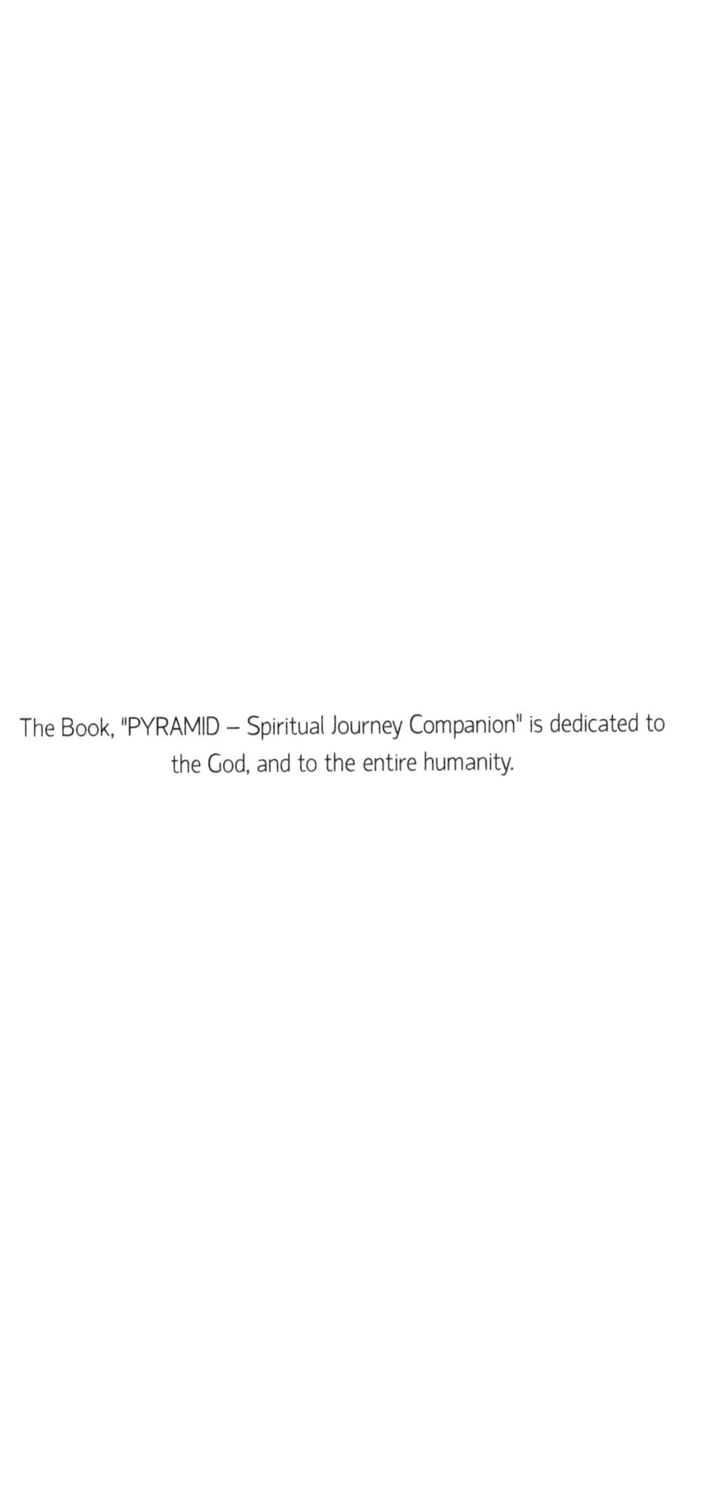

The Book, "PYRAMID – Spiritual Journey Companion" is dedicated to the God, and to the entire humanity.

Contents

Contents

Contents

Foreword

This Book, "PYRAMID – Spiritual Journey Companion" is a treatise on Meditation inside the Pyramid. Meditation, when done inside the Pyramid, becomes very easy, too intense and quite profound. Understand the game of the life. Life is a big adventure. Life is an experience of the soul. Earth is not our permanent home. Remember, the life is a big illusion. Life is a long dream, an ongoing test, but a continuous celebration. In the continuous journey of life, not everything will happen, as per the expectations. Carry a happy-go-lucky attitude in the life for success, prosperity, peace and the happiness. The size of a problem depends on one's ability to solve it. There is always a better strategy than the one, which you currently have. Keep looking up, as it is the secret of the life. Witness or observe the life. Be a spectator of the game of the life. Life is a grand show, directed by the God, played on the world stage. Either, we are the actors, or the spectators, of this grand pre-scripted play, at different moments, and in different journeys. No one is really good, and no one is really bad, as every being acts strictly as per the script and according to the time and the space coordinates. In the meditation, one gets the answer to the question, "What is the purpose of my life?" Find the answer yourself, and lead the life, as told by the universe during the meditation. Be a spiritual sculptor. Life is a dream. Life is a book. Life is the knowledge.

This Book, "PYRAMID – Spiritual Journey Companion" deals with topics like Life, Death, God, Mind, Memory. Pyramids and their Science, Yoga, Meditation and its types, Angel Numbers, Twin Flame etc., which are very essential for an awakened, meaningful, fulfilling and happy life.

Meditation inside a Pyramid is classic instance of science meeting the nature. Pyramid has such geometry that the energy of space is converged, and also, focussed downwards. It is the reason why temples have a pyramid-shaped top. Domes also produce similar effect. Meditation improves one's integrity and the quality of consciousness. Meditation gives everything in the life. Yogasana and Meditation alter electrochemical activity of the nervous system. Yogasana and Meditation, i.e. Meditation Asanas have special effects on glands and internal organs. Meditation is the higher state of Yoga.

The Author of this Book, "PYRAMID – Spiritual Journey Companion", has put all his experiences and the understanding on this topic in a very lucid manner. Readers will find it a very interesting book on this rare topic of Pyramid with the perspective of Spirituality. This Book, "PYRAMID – Spiritual Journey Companion", has many takeaways for their direct implementation in our daily life. This Book, "PYRAMID – Spiritual Journey Companion", is a treasure trove, a very precious gift to the entire humanity by the Author. The Author has done his devoir right well.

- **Baba**

22 / 03 /2023

Preface

This Book, "PYRAMID – Spiritual Journey Companion" is a very simple and comprehensive discussion on the topics, Life, Death, God, Mind, Memory. Pyramids and their Science, Yoga, Meditation and its types, Angel Numbers, Twin Flame etc., Life is a big adventure. Life is an experience of the soul. Do not hate the beings, which envy you, as those are the beings, which have accepted that you are much better than them. Every being comes with certain sunshine, display it, prove worthy of it. Our answers display our knowledge, but our questions reflect our thinking. Keep smiling no matter what. Smile opens up the heart, exhibits warmth and the oomph, and expresses love, joy, happiness, and the compassion for others. When the things inside, change, things around, also change. In the life, form a right attitude. Love and affection, and the behaviour of being, is the strongest magnet to attract any being, anything and the everything. Life is all about a right attitude. What you love, achieve it, and what you have already achieved, love it. Peace comes, when the power of love, overcomes the love for the power. Living a "big life" is far meaningful than living a "long life". Death is the time for the soul to take rest, and to, sleep, re-evaluate, recharge and rejuvenate. Death is a divine pause, a hiatus, in the soul's infinite journey. Each embryo has its own unique genetic identity, and beauty. Every being is born with unique astrological settings. Life should be "big", and not "long". Problems never stay long and along. Be aware of life's goods, and beware of surrounding evils. Problems come, put its signature in the experience book, called "the life", and then go away for good. No matter how efficient you are, if you are not on the right path, problem can never be solved. Problems never repeat in the life. Every time, there is a new problem, encountered in the journey of the life. Problems come, not to make the being weak, but strong and stronger. Problems are the opportunities of the life, opportunity to learn, opportunity to gather experiences, opportunity to become strong, and opportunity to grow. Be unstoppable and invincible. Raise the level of thoughts, let the soul evolve. Soul must evolve in every journey of life. Pyramids are not just structures, but much more beyond that. A looking or glance at / of these Pyramids, creates different vibration and feelings. Pyramids are weird and bizarre structures. Pyramids of Egypt are one of the seven Wonders of World. Pyramids prophesy major events of the planet. Some Pyramids also display time and the calendar. Probably, Pyramids of Gaza, Egypt were being used as the source of electricity. Pyramids have several layers. Pyramids have a single vertex at the top, i.e. an apex, and such a vertically converging structure always has the ability of amplifying the vibrations and the energy. The apex of the pyramid generates a Spin Field.

Meditation, when done inside the Pyramid, becomes very easy, too intense and quite profound. Pyramid is an epitome of amalgamation of science, religion and the spirituality. There are revelations of unknown secrets of the life and the universe to the meditative being during the Meditation inside the Pyramid.

This Book, "PYRAMID – Spiritual Journey Companion" is a great gift from the Author to the entire humanity in today's tough times. This Book, "PYRAMID – Spiritual Journey Companion" is a best pick of its times from the bookstores, and a must read for all. I wish all the readers, a happy reading experience, while going through, every word, every line, every paragraph, and every chapter, of it. Power is always of the soul. A well managed mind creates good and meaningful experiences of the life. Mind is managed through Meditation. Meditation inside the Pyramid is very effective. Build a Pyramid at your house in an open and peaceful area. Do Meditation inside the Pyramid and get empowered. Readings will find this book too involving, and while reading the book, the readers will feel an evolving experience within. Readers will not be able to stop reading this book, and repeating this book's reading time and again. Read and explain the chapters of the book to the members of the family, relatives and friends, and the others. Gift the Book, "PYRAMID – Spiritual Journey Companion" to them, and to the other. A gift of knowledge is the best gift.

- **Dr. Yaduvir Singh**
25 / 02 / 2023

Acknowledgements

The contents of this Book, "PYRAMID – Spiritual Journey Companion" are the results of learning, understandings, knowledge and the experiences of the Author. However, one may always differ from that, what is written here. Also, the Author tenders his earnest apologies in anticipation, if any content, hurts the reader(s), and / or is contrary to his / her / their, faith, belief, tenets, knowledge, information, and the experiences. The Author can never dare or intend to hurt the sentiments of anybody in any manner. With the folded hands, Author pleads all forgiveness from the reader, in all such cases, if found, by the reader. The author disclaims any liability, responsibility, loss, harm or damage or any other, and reading this Book is the sole discretion of the reader.

The Author will like to acknowledge, all the visible and the invisible powers of the existence, for inspiration, guidance and the motivation, encouragement and the support, hand-holding, and instilling the confidence, while the preparation of this marvel. With a deep sense of gratitude, the Author acknowledges all the visible and the invisible powers of the existence, for the confidence, information, knowledge, experiences, and the understanding provided.

The Author will like to acknowledge all the sources of information, inspiration, which gradually developed Author's understanding over many years, along with the experiences.

Last but not the least, and also, much above everything and all, nothing is possible without God's will and hand. Author with full servility, respect and the gratitude,

surrenders to the God, and puts this Book, "PYRAMID –
Spiritual Journey Companion" on the holy feet of the God.
All is of the God only.

Prologue

This Book, "PYRAMID - Spiritual Journey Companion", is a gem in itself, a marvellous intellectual creation, par excellence, and a must read Book for all, and also, a much worthy collection. It is an ideal gift on occasions. It is a very rare topic Book on, Pyramid, Life, Death, Mind, Memory, God, Meditation, Yoga, Twin Flame, Angel Numbers, Reiki, Power of Aum, Astral Travel, Time Travel etc.. Life is all about a right attitude. What you love, achieve it, and what you have already achieved, love it. Peace comes, when the power of love, overcomes the love for the power. Living a "big life" is far meaningful than living a "long life". Death is the time for the soul to take rest, and to, sleep, re-evaluate, recharge and rejuvenate. Death is a divine pause, a hiatus, in the soul's infinite journey. Each embryo has its own unique genetic identity, and beauty. Every being is born with unique astrological settings. Life should be "big", and not "long". Problems never stay long and along. Be aware of life's goods, and beware of surrounding evils. Problems come, put its signature in the experience book, called "the life", and then go away for good. Pyramid has such geometry that the energy of space is converged, and also, focussed downwards. It is the reason why temples have a pyramid-shaped top. Domes also produce similar effect. Meditation improves one's integrity and the quality of consciousness. Meditation gives everything in the life. Yogasana and Meditation alter electrochemical activity of the nervous system. Pyramid is not just an ordinary structure, but a very magical and quite a miraculous edifice. Meditation connects the meditative being with the universe and its powers. Divine knowledge descends on the meditative being, and the meditative being gains more wisdom. Meditation, when done inside the Pyramid, becomes very easy, too intense and quite profound. Pyramid is an epitome of amalgamation of science, religion and the spirituality. There are revelations of unknown secrets of the life and the universe to the meditative being during the Meditation inside the Pyramid. Successful beings do Meditation inside the Pyramid. By reading Book, "PYRAMID - Spiritual Journey Companion", actually you will not be reading this book, rather, this book will be reading you, and then, this Book will give you back everything, what you need / desire, in / from your life. The readers will find this Book, "PYRAMID - Spiritual Journey Companion", too involving, interesting, informative, and also, recreational. Books are the best friends of human beings. Books make a reader travel through all its contents, and experience the whole journey of reading him or herself even without lifting the feet. Loosen up, and lose yourself in this Book, "PYRAMID - Spiritual Journey Companion", find yourself there, nd get benefitted in the life. Keep learning, and stay healthy and happy in the life.

CHAPTER ONE

Life

Life is the preparation for a good death. Life is an examination. Draw inspiration from the existence. Live the way the nature exists. Inspire yourself to achieve all your set goals of the life. Bless yourself with peace. Bestow yourself with eternal joy and the happiness. Do not create a new karma tie. Accumulation of past karmic ties (Karma Bandh) is the reason for birth-death-rebirth, and its cycle. As you sow, so shall you reap; it is the law of nature. We create our own life. We create our own destiny. The type of karma done, creates the type of destiny. Shed off the karmic burdens. Live a life replete of exuberance and freedom. It is all a drama, going on here, in this existence. Do not take the life seriously. No event here is for real. It is a continuously changing cosmos, and change is the only constant here. Life is an opportunity; opportunity to, do the best, become the best, and get or achieve the best. Earn honestly and righteously. Chant the name of the God. Share the wealth with those, who are in need. With the pen of heart, and the ink of love, and using the intellect as the writer, write that, which has no end or the limit. Never worry for anything in the life. Let the worrying become thinking and planning. Problems never stay long. Problems come, put the signature in the experience book, known as the life, and then move away. The secret of success is right attitude, positive thinking and belief in the self. Trials and tribulations in the life do not come to punish us, but to awaken us. Stop overthinking. Overthinking is one of the biggest causes of unhappiness in the life. Keep the self occupied. Keep the mind off the things, which do not help. Always think positive. If there is a desire for peace and silence in the life, silence the desires. Unwanted desires are the cause of disturbed minds. Live the life fair and square. Never look back, as looking back, may give regrets. Always look ahead, as looking ahead, brings opportunities. Be kind. Appreciate all little and big things, which come on the way, during the journey of the life. Smile. Smile is the sacred gift of the life. Stay humble and modest. Do good for self and to others. God is always with us in the very ordinary. We are never alone in the life. Spirits always accompany us. God's ways are better than our ways. God's plans are bigger and better than our plans, and the only right ones. God's plan for the life is more fulfilling and rewarding. Stay open, and let the God do the things his ways. Do not chew on the mistakes of self, or on mistakes of the others, forgive the self, and forgive the others. Forget the bad. Do not get stuck to anything. Love the self and the others. Love makes one to blossom from inside. It is the mantra of a happy and fulfilled life. Do not entangle yourself in every matter, as setting the things right is the right of the time, and let the time only handle it. Life is always better, when we are with good beings. Try choosing the right path. Spend time in the nature. Observe the silence. Engage in prayers. Celebrate the life. Wisdom is to bring the celebrations to the life. Life always moves in the right direction. In the journey of the life, rough roads will come, as it is the design of the life by the God, for each one of us, without an exception, but they will always lead us towards a much improved and better life every time. True happiness is finding the happiness in the happiness of others. Keep moving in the life with commitment. Do Yoga, Meditation, Sudarshan Kriya and Bhastrika Pranayama; as it raises the Pranic Energy (life energy or the life force). Work on seven Chakras. Change your breathing patterns, as doing so, changes the whole life, and its associated patterns. Do not value privileges over principles; otherwise, one loses the both. One of the hardest things to do, is to let go, what was thought to be real. Knowing is being. All is an illusion, and illusion is the only reality here, in this God's creation. One is never ever alone in the journey of life, in all of its forms, whether physical or the spirit. The God, the universe and the nature, are the biggest teachers. A teacher is a garbage collector. There is no better designer than the nature. Live fearlessly. In the game of the life, what goes around, definitely comes around. Understand the game of the life. Life is a big adventure. Life is an experience of the soul. Do not hate the beings, which envy you, as those are the beings, which have accepted that you are much better than them. Every being comes with certain sunshine, display it, prove worthy of it. Our answers display our knowledge, but our questions reflect our thinking. Keep smiling no matter what. Smile opens up the heart, exhibits warmth and the oomph, and expresses love, joy, happiness, and the compassion for others. When the things inside, change, things around, also change. In the life, form a right attitude. Love and affection, and the behaviour of being, is the strongest magnet to attract any being, anything and the everything. Life is all about a right attitude. What you love, achieve it, and what you have already achieved, love it. Peace comes, when the power of love, overcomes the love for the power. Living a "big life" is far meaningful than living a "long life". One should have, the friends which care, neighbours which understand pains, relatives which respect, and the family which loves. The greatest discovery in the life is to discover own faults, and the greatest virtue is to accept and say openly that I was wrong. Desires in the life, should not dictate the life. Do not work on the life, but work on the self. Do not try making the life easy, but try making the self strong enough for it. Right time never comes in the life, but the time has to be set right by us, with rights thoughts, right choices, right decisions, and the right actions. Right endeavours lead us to better life. History says that the past was good; science says that the future will be good, whereas, the religion and the spirituality say, if heart is pure and the mind is at peace, happiness is just now and here, in this very moment, and today. Expectations break, but the hope and belief persist; is the beauty of the life. Do good to others, as it comes back, in many unexpected and inexplicable ways. Being's every act and the motion, in the life, must be the poetry in motion. Learn patience, as it makes the life easier. Perfect ending to every day of the life is to finish strong. Sometimes, one should leave, not for ego, but for the self-respect. Self-respect is the feeling of confidence and the pride, in the self. Integrity is a desideratum in the life. Develop, and maintain a strong character through thick and thin. Lucubrate for intellectual, scholarly, social, religious and spiritual works. Carry a happy-go-lucky attitude in the life for success, prosperity, peace and the happiness. The size of a problem depends on one's ability to solve it. There is always a better strategy than the one, which you currently have. Keep looking up, as it is the secret of the life. Witness or observe the life. Be a spectator of the game of the life. Life is a grand show, directed by the God, played on the world stage. Either, we are the actors, or the spectators, of this grand pre-scripted play, at different moments, and in different journeys. No one is really good, and no one is really bad, as every being acts strictly as per the script and according to the time and the space coordinates. In the meditation, one gets the answer to the question, "What is the purpose of my life?" Find the answer yourself, and lead the life, as told by the universe during the meditation. Be a spiritual sculptor. Life is a dream. Life is a book. Life is the knowledge. Life should exist. And, the life should be easy. Life should be led consciously. Life should not be accidental. Keep a smile on the face, always. Be happy and make others happy in the life. A weak being can never forgive the other(s). Only a strong being can forgive the other(s). In the journey of the life, be frank and straight to the self, and also, to the others, and call a spade a spade. Real happiness does not lie in the money. Always do that, what makes you happy. Stay healthy and peaceful. Prioritise the things to be done in the life. Journey of life is too short. Earth is not our permanent home. Remember, the life is a big illusion. Life is a long dream, an ongoing test, but a continuous celebration. In the continuous journey of life, not everything will happen, as per the expectations. Do not expect anything from anyone. Drop the expectations in order to stay happy, and to live happily, and go with the flow of the life and flow as it goes. Expectations are quite hurtful. Comparisons are very painful. Why to make life miserable by expecting or by comparing? We are the architects of our own life. We all had been in this present life form and the innumerable other life forms, for donkey's years. Come out of this trap and the loop. Always feel happy. Happiness is the best feeling, the gift of the God. Be happy and keep smiling.

This physical life is too short. Love the life. Before speaking, always listen to others. Before writing something, think. Before spending, earn. Before praying the God, forgive the others. Before getting hurt, feel the reality. Before hating, love the things. Before quitting, try the thing to the best of your given ability. And, before dying, live. Live the life. Problems are the part of the life, so is the design of the life; and facing these problems with aplomb and a big smile, is the art of the life. Life is not about the quantity, but about its quality. Getting to know that someone is happy because of me, is one of the best feelings. Always be happy, not because everything is going good in the life, but because, you can see "the good" in everything presented to the life. Life is all about thoughts (सोच), ideas (विचार) and the perception (धारणा). Success breeds success. In the grand show of the life, only truth prevails, and rest all ends. Mother's is the most important physical, and also, the spiritual relation of the life. Value this relation, and also other relations, of the journey of life. True relations and relationships are connected to you, and not connected with the time. Mother is solace. Mother is relief. Try exploring, whether you are the whole creation, or you are mere an element in this vast creation. Life is a game of time. It is all about time. The change of time, changes the world. Relationships, which are based on changed time, are simply fake. Most of the relationships are feigned. Be into a true relationship. Caring is sharing. Care and love, in order to create a right kind of the relationship. True love always has intimacy, passion and commitment in the mind. Real relationships exist in both, viz. the good and the bad times, during the journey of life. Such beings, which stay and support during the bad times of the life, are angels. Respect the self. What you have, many others can have too, but what you are, no other being can be. We all are born blessed. Every time a hand must reach out to help the other being. Put anger aside, and strive for understanding. Forget the differences, and realise the love within, for each other. Mistake increases the experience, and the experience decreases the mistakes. Take it easy, make it easy. Do not forget living the life, while chasing the dreams of the life. Values are most important valuables. In the show of the life, a leader is a being, whose actions, inspire the others to, dream more, learn more, do more, and become more. Life is sacred, because life and the creation manifest the God. Therefore, life and the creation are the places of encounter with the God. Life is an outcome of, series of decisions and actions to, build, test, change, iterate, and create, something new, every time. Always thank the self, for how far you have come in the journey of the life. The journey of the life was never easy. But, the self has always mustered up the courage, and gathered the strength, to continue to move forward in the journey of the life, and face the challenges of the life. To be the best in the life, one must be able to handle the worst in the life. Life is a balance between holding on the things, and also, letting go off the things. What to hold, and what to let off, creates the kind of the life; the quality of life. Empty stomach i.e. being peckish, and penury i.e. no money or broke, and the broken heart i.e. being jilted, teach the best lessons of life. Life is rough, so you have got to be tough. As the dirty waters do not stop the plants from growing, similarly, let the negative words spoken by the others do not stop or thwart you from making progress. Colours of happiness and joy are most beautiful colours of the life. Life is a festival of colours, full of happiness. In the journey of life, never cut a thing, that can be untied. Never stop chasing the dreams, as we never know, when, how and where, life will take you from state of zero to a state of hero in a fraction of time. Beings want more and more time in life, but, mostly use it in the worst ways. That being suffers more than the necessary, which starts suffering, before it is necessary. For inner peace and the happiness, learn to ignore the things. In the end, we all, and everything which had existed at that time, simply become short-lived memories and the stories; so is the life. Journey of life, is essentially, a journey in the time through the space. We all are time-travellers. Some of us may be living their present in the present times, whereas, few other beings might be living their past in the present times, and remaining others beings might be living their future in the present times. It is the reason, why we come at different time, and also, go at the different time. Beings, which like or are satisfied with the present bad times, might be travelling their past in the present times. Beings, which dislike present bad times, might be travelling their future in the present times. As Bhootkaal (Past time) had existed and is also present in the memory, so Bhoot (Ghosts) also exist, and are present. Every journey of life is essentially a preparation for the next journey of the life. In the epic drama of the life, and of the existence, always support the truth and what is right, and call spade a spade. Lead a very simple life with utmost simplicity, as simplicity is the ultimate sophistication, and the biggest attraction. Weave intention into the action. Think very little anent the life. Things that challenges us, also changes us. In the life, there should not be any expectation of how things should or shouldn't be, but there is only "things as they are." The experience of living the life must be very vast and expansive, and less dependent on the false identities, which the mind thinks of us to be. Actions govern the existence. Things that we wish for, or want in our life, are on the other side of our fear(s). Allay all fears in order to celebrate the life. Get au fait with the design of the life with the help of Yoga and the Meditation, and the tools like Pyramid, the spiritual journey companion.

CHAPTER TWO

Death

Death is necessary for the existence to exist. Death is a change. Death is a transition, a movement from one room to another. Death is a celebration. Death is liberation from the mundane and the monotonous. Death must be seamless. Die in the state of spiritual consciousness. Change is the very nature of the existence. Nothing dies here, nor is it born. We all had existed from the day and the time of creation of this existence, and will keep existing till the existence exits. God has created both, the birth and the death. How something created by the God, can be questionable? Everything created by the God is just perfect. If there is no death, how new relations will be created and experienced. Life is for experiencing new and the newest. We are energies, and energy can neither be created nor be destroyed. A well-lived life leads to dying well. The tragedy of life is not the death, but the resources within, that die, when still being alive; use it or lose it. Life and its design must be understood by all for a happy and successful journey of the life. Death is the time for the soul to take rest, and to, sleep, re-evaluate, recharge and rejuvenate. Death is a divine pause, a hiatus, in the soul's infinite journey. Each embryo has its own unique genetic identity, and beauty. Every being is born with unique astrological settings. Life should be "big", and not "long". Problems never stay long and along. Be aware of life's goods, and beware of surrounding evils. Problems come, put its signature in the experience book, called "the life", and then go away for good. No matter how efficient you are, if you are not on the right path, problem can never be solved. Problems never repeat in the life. Every time, there is a new problem, encountered in the journey of the life. Problems come, not to make the being weak, but strong and stronger. Problems are the opportunities of the life, opportunity to learn, opportunity to gather experiences, opportunity to become strong, and opportunity to grow. Be unstoppable and invincible. Raise the level of thoughts, let the soul evolve. Soul must evolve in every journey of life. Every soul in the afterworld upon death gets a Psychopomp. Psychopomp is the conductor of the souls. Dying thoughts are carried to the next birth. Death can be well-understood through meditation. One of the life's tragedies is that we get old too soon, and get wise too late. Common beings fail to jerry, what is the life, what is the purpose of life, why different events take place in the life. Everything is important, which exists here in the creation, and one should never play down it. Death must be graceful. Death is the change of the costume of the soul. Death is the change of the location for the soul. Death is the ultimate reality. Death is a painful truth at the psychological level - a familiar pang of heartache. Death is a sleep-state, and the sleep is always caring, relaxing, endearing and healing, in its nature. Both, birth and death are simply the passages of the time. Birth is a beautiful lie. We are never born, and never dead.

CHAPTER THREE

Mind

The sensate world is essentially mind's world. Life is all about mind management. Pain and pleasure are two of many dual creations of the mind. Let the mind work for you, and not the mind dictate you. Subdue, or conquer over, the mind by practising Yoga and Meditation; as these techniques keep the mind peaceful. Quieten the mind, and let the soul to speak. Do Yoga and Meditation regularly. A being's brain is simply a frequency analyser, as it picks up the frequencies from the environment and the universe, analyses and concludes it, and also, sends certain frequencies back into the universe for the thoughts created and the actions performed. We all are vibrations. God is also a vibration, the supreme vibration. We all are energies, simply energy. God is also energy. Vibrations create reality. In the case of normal beings, mind creates more pains than the pleasures. Never identify the self with the desire(s), as it will then make the life very miserable. Life never controls a being, but, his or her thought(s), control(s) his or her life, and make the kind of life. Beings suffer more in their imagination(s), than in the reality. Always be mindful. Live in the state of consciousness. Majority of beings lead and live their lives unconsciously and accidentally. A conscious thought and action, avoid making any new karma. Do not create karma. Karma creates the trap, the trap of birth, death and then rebirth, and the cycle of karma-trap goes on and on for good. Integrity is the characteristic of consciousness. Conscious living is the only purpose of the life. Life is kinda funny. In this God's world, there is nothing like success and the failure, but everything is a continuum of events; the infinite life process. Beings have created the definitions of success and failure. Success is never an accident in the life. Perceived success is always the result of faith and the hard work. Faith, trust, belief, love, respect, compassion and hope, are the essence of the life. A peaceful mind is the real treasure of the life. Life is infinite, and not just the few years. There is a certain afterlife. Life is physical, as well as spiritual, i.e. in the spirit form. We become, what we live around. We all are one, and not different. All species have come from the same source. I am just another you. What we hold in the mind, sooner or later occurs in the life. What is sent, comes back. We all, and the everything, in this universe, are connected through the minds; it is a simple science. Use the power of the subconscious mind for success and meaningful life. A certain portion of the mind travels from one birth to the other. Our innate likes and dislikes, attractions and abhorrence, skills, are carry forwarded by the mind from previous birth to this birth, or this birth to next birth. Mind is the memory; an imprint of thoughts and actions on the being's energy landscape. Brain is not the mind. Also, consciousness is not the mind. Certain traits and qualities, which travel along with the consciousness, is the mind. Mind is all over the body of the being, and not at any one place inside the body. Mind is the spiritual element of the memory and the intellect. Mind is energy. Everything in this creation is energy. All manifestations are created out of a certain proportionate mix of the energy and the matter. Beings are nature's manifestation. Universe is also energy. The quality of the life is created by us only, and it begins with, how we choose to think. For every problem, as confronted in the life, tell the mind, that there lies a best solution, and the mind will then find it for you; it is a secret, not known to many. It is the basis of the Law of Attraction. Use the mind as the slave, and do not let it become the master of the life. Hold the mind, and stop it from wandering, as otherwise, it will bring forth problem(s). A wandering mind is like a mad elephant, simply destructive; otherwise it is a tamed lion, if controlled. Limitations are the creations of the mind. Train the mind so as to see the good, in everything. Use your superego. Superego is the part of a mind, which acts as a self-critical conscience, and thus, reflects the social standards learned from parents and teachers, and the surrounding. We are the architects of our own lives, and the mind is the tool for it. Our realities of the life, i.e. the repeated patterns of behaviour and emotions, are rooted in the subconscious mind. Universe surrenders before a still mind. Mind creates the quality of being's thoughts and actions. Mind is positive, and also, negative. Mind is everything. Thoughts are created in the mind. We are reflection of our thoughts. Let the mind, do not create sufferings, in the life. Peace in the life is a certain state of the mind. Mind creates a lack of perspective, i.e. a suitable perspective, as otherwise, everything happening in the creation is just beautiful, rational, logical, and simply wholesome. The universe has a much greater responsibility than any one of us to keep the life and the show of the life, and the play of the creation, going in much better ways. Everything, which happens in the life, whether controlled or uncontrolled, is for good. Accept, and do not expect. Mind is the element, which enables one to become aware of the world around, and to experience, to think, and to feel. Mind is the faculty of the consciousness and the thoughts. Mind is the ability to think and to reason, i.e. the intellect. Unnecessary inside chattering is wrong. Do not speak, and the peace will prevail upon you. Nature's intelligence drives us. Nature's intelligence is inside and outside us. Keep the mind open. Expand the mind. There are three types of minds, viz. the conscious mind, the subconscious mind, and the unconscious mind. Buddhi, Manas, Ahankara and Chitta are the four parts of the mind. Mind and the body are not two separate entities. Body is the gross form of the mind. Mind is the subtle form of the body. Body must be full of vitality and strength. Mind must be light and creative, joyful and balanced. Yogasana and the Meditation, integrate and harmonise, the mind and the body. Body and the mind, harbour tension, known as the knot(s). Muscular knots make the body stiff, e.g. Neuralgia, Cervical Spondylitis. For every physical muscular knot, there is a corresponding mental knot, and the vice versa. Yogasana, Pranayama, Shatkarmas, Yog Nidra and Meditation, open-up these knots, and release the trapped dormant energy. Yogasana and the Meditation act directly at the physical level on the body, and then from the body to the mind, somato-psychically way indirectly. One should never be the product of his or her circumstances of the life, but the product of his or her decisions taken, and thoughtful actions performed in the life. Sustained habits become part of the DNA. Time does not change the life, but changes the expiry dates of life's opportunities. In order to live in peace, help others to live in peace. In order to get loved, love others. In order to live well, help others to live well.

The value of the life lived, is measured by the lives touched. Happiness is organic, and is intertwined with the welfare of others. Happiness is a choice and not any result. Nothing makes us happy, until we choose to be happy. No being can make us happy, unless we decide to be happy. Happiness does not come to us, but it comes from us. Use the moments of the life, in order to grow, as otherwise you will lose it. Unused time dies. Unused talent diminishes. Unused potential decays. Unused knowledge becomes a burden eventually. What is not used, is abused. If opportunity does not knock, build a door. Helping others is helping self. Keep doing all little things, unstoppably in the life, as these little things occupy much bigger proportions of the hearts. Enjoy every little thing in the life, for one day, you shall look back, and then remorsefully realise that it was really big. Tell the mind, you are my slave.

CHAPTER FOUR

Memory

Time is derived from memory. Memory is a part of mind. Mind accompanies consciousness. Thus, time will always move along with the consciousness. Past is a memory. Past life is also a memory. Time creates the memory. Memories create the time. Memory is karma. Karma is memory. Memory is the ability of the energy to store the patterns, patterns of behaviour. Cosmic intelligence is based on cosmic memory. Nature has memorised all of its processes. Cell has memory. In the root of the memory, there is dependence, and the love, the unconditional love. Our aptitude and attitude are memories. Memory creates the notions of parents, family, relations, friends, colleagues, society, state, nation, the world, and the God. God is an outcome of memory. A being that has no memory, will have no notions of anything, no time, no space. Memory creates pleasures and pains. Work on the mind, in order to control the memory in your favour. Memory creates the kind of life. Good memories will create a good life and bad memories will create a bad life, if there is no comparison of past and present situations and circumstances. There are eight types of memories, viz. conscious, unconscious, articulate, inarticulate, karmic, elemental, atomic and the genetic. Life is a question of choice(s). Life is a question of option(s). So, what is being chosen or opted makes the kind of life. Memory is a source of pain for the normal beings. If there is bad memory, pain is felt. And, if there is a good memory of the past, there is dissatisfaction that present is not that good, leading to wistful longings, yearning and nostalgia. It is good that beings forget, otherwise, it is not possible to undertake the further journey of the life with all the memories of the past. If the load of accessible memories is being increased, the being will become insane. A being, whose intellect sees everything, mere as a play of the life, and also, he or she does not stick to any action or an event or a circumstance, then he or she does not create any new karma. It is called the conscious living. Have a control over the mind, in order to access the memory, in a full conscious manner. Meditation controls the mind. As far as memories went, let the mind tell that this one was a lulu. Storage is the basic nature of energy, so memory exists along with the consciousness. Interpretation of memory is done by the mind. Everything is just an event in the life, creating an experience for the soul for soul's evolution, and it is neither good nor bad, and thus, no memory is either good or bad. Let the mind fetch a memory for creating good thought(s) leading to good action(s). Memory contains the experiences, i.e. the experiences of the life. Karma is memory. Life is all about experiencing. And this experiencing, leads to the evolution of soul, and the growth of being's consciousness. Ultimately, the consciousness has to improve anyways, as the consciousness has to come to a certain level of quality, i.e. purity, in order to come out of the trap or the loop, and breaking the shackles of the bondages of the life, birth, death and rebirth; it is the state of Moksha or the Nirvana. Memory heals. A life, which touches others, goes on forever, and breaks all bounds of the memory.

CHAPTER FIVE

Absence Of Evidence Is Not Evidence Of Absence

Currently, it is the Dark Age. Dark Age is a time during which things in general and the civilisation in particular undergo a sharp decline. Some beings believe in the existence of the God, but they do not listen to the God at all, in their created thought(s) and reflected action(s). Absence of evidence is not evidence of absence. Beings have limited sense-perception capability. Air, light and smell cannot be sense-perceived directly, but their created effect(s) can only be sense-perceived, to a limited extent. There is certain limit or threshold of sense-perception for every being, and below that limit or threshold of sense, no object or event cannot be sense-perceived. Eagle has better eyes than us, ants and bees have better olfactory ability than us, snakes have better vibration picking ability than us, and bats can listen to much higher frequencies than us. Bats produce echolocation by emitting very high frequency sound pulses. These pulses are produced by the bats through their mouth or nose. And then, bats listen to the echo, so created by the pulse rebound. With this echo, bats determine the size, shape and texture of objects present in its environment. Owls can see in the night. There is a full night world, similar to the day world. There are both, diurnal and nocturnal beings in this cosmos. There is a complete terrestrial world, and also, there is a complete underwater world. It is never the case that something which cannot be sense-perceived, does not exist. Energy directly can never be sense-perceived, but only its created effect(s) are sense-perceived. Energy manifests itself in the form of effect(s). God is energy. We are energies. God can be experienced through the experience of effect(s) produced by the God energy. Matter can be sense-perceived directly unlike the energy. To create effect(s), energy associates itself with matter, and then manifests itself in the form of event(s), and the application(s). We are always accompanied by many spirits during the journey of life. The beings, which can act as the medium, can directly sense-perceive the presence of such spirits. Such beings are able to communicate and hold conversations with these spirits. Every being has different level of sense-perception ability. It depends upon his or her level of consciousness. It is the reason, why every being has his or her, own world. World is the set of life experiences. No two beings have similar world, and also, similar life. The kind of a life, a being leads, depends upon his or her level of consciousness. Sharpening the power of attention, and the power of concentration, sharpens the sense-perception(s). Yoga and Meditation sharpen sense-perception. Live at a higher level of consciousness. At a better and higher level of consciousness, sense of unification, and the happiness, automatically develop and prevail. We all beings are same, and not different, for each one of us has same God's element within us, the soul. We are complete universe. We create this universe. We are the gods. God is only our understanding. Any pure energy is simply divine and godlike. Pure energy is all benevolent, loving, caring, merciful, protecting and guarding. Life is blissful, if lived at a higher level of consciousness. In this whole creation, there is only love, and the pure love. Creation cannot sustain without love. Power of love is unmatched, and simply unparallel. Be a paragon. God is pure love. In the game of life, what is being given, is only returned. If love is given, love will be returned. And if, anger and hate are given, same will be returned. Money does not bring peace, joy and the happiness in the life, rather it takes both away. Money is means, and not the goal. Good quality of thought(s), and good action(s), bring peace, joy and the happiness in the life. Mind becomes calm, quite and positive, with Yoga and the Meditation. Thoughts are created in the mind. Positive thinking is quite powerful. Only positive thinking brings success and the peace, joy and the happiness, in the life. Never every deny, which does not exist in the sense-perception. Say, it is not yet in my experience(s). Life changes every day, rather every moment. What is not there at this moment, may come or happen or appear or manifest, in the very next moment of the journey of the life. Life is a riddle with eddies; more and more, one tries solving it, more and more, he or she gets tangled up in it. Do not be serious about the life, just be sincere towards the life, and keep moving with the flow of the time. Life is a graph on time-space plane. Life is an infinite journey. All physical and material will be left back here on earth, the physical world. Except the unconditional love, nothing is constant here and going to exist, no relationship, no wealth, just nothing. Love travels though the time and the space. Lead a conscious life. A consciously led life is only a meaningful life. Life is an opportunity; an opportunity, to develop and to grow spiritually. Therefore, do not miss this opportunity of developing and growing. We all are here to help one another. We are caretakers of the divine property. We all, just everything, the birds, trees, animals, rivers, mountains, sky etc., is one big family, i.e. the God's family. God is the head of this family. God is omnipresent and omnipotent, then why to worry. Just keep moving in the journey of the life, with trust on others, and belief and faith in the self, and in the God. God is always with us no matter what. We all have a Guardian Spirit. This Guardian Spirit is God sent, to assist us, during the journey of life. Respect one another. Disrespecting others is disrespecting the God. Shower all your love and care on the others, especially those, who need your help. God helps many through few. Provide all possible succour. Those who help the others, God helps them. Magic and miracles happen in the life. For you and me, being alive at this moment, is also a miracle, a magic of the God. Befriend the nature. While giving help and the advice, act like a father, and while showing pity and compassion, and showering the love and affection, act like a mother. This creation is ours and yours. I am the creation. We are the creation. The creation of the God exists, because I and you exist. As this creation will always exist, so I and you and we all shall exist always. We are eternal. We are immortal. Be human. Be humane. Being human, is the only merit of the life, and the God's only blessing in the life. Never insist for proofs, as proof(s) may not be produced instantly, but for sure, proof(s) will be presented, just wait for an appropriate time and space in the journey of life. One, who seeks, for sure, gets all answers. Become a seeker. Life is an answer, and not a question. Life is an attitude, a perspective. Develop a right attitude, i.e. a right perspective, in order to live a meaningful and a very happy life. Accept, if convinced, what comes your way, but reject, only after exercising full prudence, as what is being rejected, may not come back again, in the journey of the life. Dreams do not work, unless you do.

CHAPTER SIX

The God And The Pyramid

God is the supreme energy of the whole existence. God is in the nucleus of this whole existence or the whole creation, and rest everything, is just orbiting around the God, in differently graded orbits, depending upon its level of consciousness. God is the supreme consciousness. Consciousness is the energy. This whole creation, and everything in it, is just energy. God's way is always better than our ways. God's plan is always bigger than our plan, God's design for our life is always more rewarding, more fulfilling, and better, than what we have ever dreamed of. Stay open, and let the God do it, his way. In the physical body, God can only be experienced, but in the spirit form, God can be reached or accessed. God can only be reached, when the thoughts of being are quintessential pure and immaculate. Physical body cannot contain a very high level soul or spirit. God is not the matter, but the energy. In this creation, and in every created thing, there is an element of God's energy inside. Nothing is dead here in this creation. There is no death, but life, and only life. Creation is a play of matter and energy. Everything here, contributes in the show of the life and the game of the creation. Even the assumed dead, gives birth to something here in this creation; strange. There is a concept of "dying to be born again" in the nature and this creation. The processes of nature and this creation are cyclical in their nature, i.e. loop form. And, this loop is the trap, which is caused by the karma, and this is the reason, why we are born and die, again and again. There are ways to exit this trap, which is bondage. Being's own thoughts and actions thereof, create this trap or the bondage. Soul is trapped in the body. Freedom is the nature of soul. In the state of godliness, there is no sorrow, pain or distress, but only, peace, love harmony, joy and the happiness. God created the universes. God is the supreme and the ultimate reality. God is the energy, perfect in power, wisdom, and goodness. God is the creator and ruler of the universes. "GOD" is the Generator, the Operator, and the Destroyer. The life force, present within all of us, is the element of the God, in each one of us. We are never alone. God's love and care are always there with us. We are the part of the nature, and not something, which is different from the nature. Live in sync with the nature; the nature's style. We are the, tree, birds, animals, rivers, mountains, sun, moon, planets, earth, air, light, soil, and everything. Every other created thing in this creation is our reflection. I am just another you. Prayer or the worship changes the very nature of the being, which performs it. Prayer or the worship helps change the state of that being doing or performing it. We are always resonated with the frequencies of the universe, and when this resonance is broken, we are gone. God can only be experienced and accessed in a certain state. However, God is always imperceptibly present with us, within us, all the time. Everything here in this creation has life. Life is the God. God is everywhere, in all the directions. There is nothing superior or inferior, as the God has made everything. Everything is just at its best. God is merciful and glorious. God listens to us all the time. When we pray, God listens, and when we listen, God talks, and when we believe, God works. God always has a better plan for each one us. God knows our destiny. God knows are journey of life. God is the teacher, and we are his students, sometimes rewarded, sometimes punished, but always cared, protected and loved. God always does that, what is best for each one of us. God is the greatest, show-maker and the player. The show of the universe, and the game of the life, is scripted, created and directed by the God, and played by us and his other created entities. Some ways of the God are quite strange, intriguing and inexplicable, some ways are direct and straight, and some indirect. Miracles happen. God is the best magician. God is the healer. God is solution of every problem. More and more, we believe and trust the God, more and more limitless, our possibilities become. God gave us life. God gave us things to eat. God gave us family, friends, relatives and community, days and nights, water, air and everything. Always, be thankful to this energy of the universe, called "the God". There are certain laws of this creation. God has made all these laws. God's purposes are divine. Impossible simply becomes possible with the intervention of the God. Insurmountable problem becomes surmountable problem. God is an endless hope. God never gives, any being, anything, which he or she, just cannot handle. God tests us with sending difficulties. In essence, no difficulty is a difficulty, and no pain is a pain; but a false creation by the mind. There are certain ways or methods of experiencing and reaching or accessing the God, like Mantra, Tantra, Yoga and the Meditation. There are certain tools as well, which help achieve the higher states of Yoga and the Meditation quite early and easily, so that profundity of the God may be experienced, accessed or reached. I am the divine flame. Purpose is to reach this flame, experience it and be with it. Pyramid is such a tool, which is used for deeper and easy meditation. Pyramid eases the process of experiencing the God during the meditation. Pyramid makes the paranormal experiencing process very easy, as it acts as the catalyst to the processes of Yoga and the Meditation, when being done or performed inside it. Pyramid is the companion of being's spiritual journey. Who creates and controls the breathing, who initiated first contraction and expansion of the heart, and many more others, are the questions of life, and proof and signs of the existence of the God. God is love and love is the God. Little science distances beings from the God, but more and deeper science, brings beings nearer to the God. Life smiles when you are happy, but the life salutes, when you make others happy. Help the self, and also, the others, by doing meditation inside the pyramid.

CHAPTER SEVEN

Pyramids Of Giza Egypt

The pyramids of Giza, located just outside of Cairo, Egypt, c. 2686–2325 BCE, are funerary edifices. The pyramids of Giza Egypt are the royal tombs of three different Pharaohs. Pharaoh is the title for ancient kings of Egypt. The northernmost, the largest and the oldest pyramid of the group of three pyramids of Giza was built for second king of fourth dynasty, Khufu. It is also known as the Great Pyramid. It is 147 metres high. The middle pyramid was built for fourth of the eight kings of fourth dynasty, Khafre. It is 143 metres high. And, the southernmost and last pyramid to be built was for the fifth king of fourth dynasty, Menkaure. It is 66 metres high. Near each pyramid, a mortuary temple was constructed. Each mortuary temple was linked to a valley temple through a causeway, on the edge of the Nile floodplain. To the south of the Great Pyramid, near Khafre's valley temple, there lies the Great Sphinx. The Great Shinx is carved out of limestone. The Great Sphinx has face of a man and the body of a recumbent lion. The Great Sphinx is 73 metres long and 20 metres high. The Great Sphinx is known to be a portrait statue of the king. The Great Sphinx continued as a royal portrait type throughout the Egyptian history. Pyramid of Giza, Egypt have been constructed of or faced with stones or bricks. These pyramids have rectangular bases with four sloping triangular sides meeting. Pyramids are found in Cyprus, Egypt, Ethiopia, Greece, India, Italy, Mexico, and some islands of Pacific Ocean, South America, Sudan, Thailand and the western Asia. These pyramids are mostly solid masses of stone, and very little can be found inside. There are passageways underneath each pyramid at their bases, which lead to small subterranean burial chambers. There are no hieroglyphic texts, or treasures, or mummies, in any of pyramids of Giza, Egypt. Cats and rats, which by mistake ever entered the Pyramid, were never able to come out of the Pyramid. These cats and rats used to get confused inside the Pyramid, and eventually get trapped forever inside it, and ultimately die. These cats and rats upon death, never got rotten, and also, there was no stink, but eventually got dried up, lying there like the mummies. There is a lot of humidity in the environment surrounding these Pyramids due to their nearness to the sea, but still, meat does not get rot and no fetid, but simply just dries up. There is no stink arising of this meat. Fish, if kept inside the Pyramid, does not get rot, but gets dried up. It is due to the special geometry of the Pyramid. Geometry affects the life, and also the associated life energies. Pyramid creates positive effect on the mind and the body; therefore, beings must put on their headgear of the shape of a Pyramid. Pyramids display the power of Pharaoh. Upon the death, Pharaoh's body was mummified, and then, entombed in a pyramid. Certain valuable possessions, mummified servants and pets, were also being buried, for use by the Pharaoh, in his afterlife. Pharaoh was believed to be a semi-divine being. Pharaoh ruled the earth during their physical life, and upon death, they were believed to have passed into an afterlife amongst the gods. Pharaoh served as the religious leader, as well as, the secular leader, during those times, in the Egypt. Egyptian civilisation thrived along the river Nile, as Nile's annual flooding ensured a reliable and very rich soil for growing crops. Egypt is called the "Cradle of Civilization." Egyptian civilisation had successfully developed over thousands of years. The beings of this civilisation had greatly contributed to the present day appreciation for the Mathematics, the Science, and the Art. To the mind, which is still, surrenders the universe. Life is not about the control, but about the liberation. These developments of Egyptian civilisation have incredibly influenced the human history, the religion and the spirituality.

CHAPTER EIGHT

Science Of Pyramid

Pyramids are being built with greater accuracy and precision. Electromagnetic charge is found to be quite intense at the Pyramid. Some pyramids are used for the purpose of telling the past and the present of the beings, and also, predicting their future. Pyramids are not just structures, but much more beyond that. A looking or glance at / of these Pyramids, creates different vibration and feelings. Pyramids are weird and bizarre structures. Pyramids of Egypt are one of the seven Wonders of World. Pyramids prophesy major events of the planet. Some Pyramids also display time and the calendar. Probably, Pyramids of Gaza, Egypt were being used as the source of electricity. Pyramids have several layers. Pyramids have a single vertex at the top, i.e. an apex, and such a vertically converging structure always has the ability of amplifying the vibrations and the energy. The apex of the pyramid generates a Spin Field. In a Spin Field, electrons spin on their axes, under a certain imparted angular momentum. There are traces of Quartz, being used in the slanted walls of Pyramids. Quartz crystal is naturally available. Quartz is a hard mineral composed of Silica. Quartz is chemically inert. It is heat resistant. Quartz possesses electrical property, known as Piezoelectricity. Quartz is the stone of courage. Quartz affects the mind. In the Piezoelectricity phenomenon, the crystal, when being mechanically stressed, generates potential difference between its ends, by the process of rearrangement of charges within. At the location of Pyramids, electromagnetic waves are relatively intense with high electromagnetic flux. Vibrations of Pyramids will create electricity according to the Science. The Science of Pyramids is such that Pyramids reduce pollution. Also, phases of Pyramids boost the Ozone layer. Ozone layer is found in the stratosphere approximately 15 - 30 Kilometres above the surface of the Earth. Ozone layer covers the entire Earth, and protects the life here on the Earth, by absorbing the harmful ultraviolet (UV) radiations of the Sun. Each side of Great Pyramid rises at an angle of 52 degrees 51 minutes to the top. Due to this slant angle, near maximum voltage is being achieved. The alignment of the Pyramid is always to the North. Pyramids act as a resonator of energy field. Pyramids act as the Amplifier - Receiver of energies, entering into it from its North, and leaving it from its South. The energy, after entering the Pyramid, rebounds from its walls, and thus, amplifies several times. The converging structure of the Pyramid, creates a beam formation of this amplified energy, which is directed downwards its apex, pooled or collected, so as to form fire in the middle. This energy is pooled or collected at the Centre of Mass or Centre of Gravity of the Pyramid, which is located at a height of 1/3 rd of the height of the Pyramid from its base, or 2/3 rd of the depth of the Pyramid from its apex. The atoms or molecules absorb this hugely amplified pooled energy, and start resonating. A very high voltage was produced at the apex or the tip of the Pyramid. Sun and Moon phases had an effect on the energy field of Pyramid, thus affecting the energy field of the environment, and the Laws of Nature, like the Law of Gravity, for certain time duration. Inside the Pyramid, several organic and non-organic observations are being made. Pyramids generate negative ions, which are quite conducive to the physical and mental health. These negative ions, also help in, dehydration, purification of water, maintenance of lustre and sheen of shining objects, healing, maintaining taste of food items, conservation of food stuffs. Meditation inside the Pyramid brings more relaxation and peace. Food is also been preserved for a longer time inside the Pyramids, and it does not rot or decay. Meditation inside the Pyramid brings more warmth, a perceptible sense of weightlessness, increased focussing, heightened tranquility and immense positivity. Pyramids multiple the cells, thus, foster the growth of plants and animals. Giants could have been developed in the earlier times with the help of these Pyramids. Pyramids had several religious purposes too. Egyptians believed in an afterlife. Egyptians believed that a second self, called the "ka" lived within every being. When the physical body expires, "ka" enjoys the eternal life. The shape of the Pyramid symbolises a new life to the dead. Pyramid represents the sense of life, the physical body emerging from the earth. This emerging body ascends towards the light of the sun. Pyramid symbolises bigger consciousness of strength and energy. Pyramids are the source of various mystical experiences. Pyramid is a symbol for the integration of self and the soul. Pyramid symbolises rebirth. The base of Pyramid represents the body, the sides the spiritual attempts, and the apex the harmonious union of being with the highest self, i.e. the God. There is great significance of an equilateral triangle. The three sides of an equilateral triangle refer to the tri-natured aspect of the

God, i.e. the God as the creator, the God as the preserver, and the God as the transformer. The shape of the Pyramid reflects the underlying aspects of divine unity. Pyramid has 4 faces. Three faces of Pyramid are directing towards the heavens, and the remaining one face of Pyramid directs towards the Earth. Pyramid is composed of 4 equilateral triangles. These equilateral triangles manifest the cosmic nature of the God, i.e. 3 in 1 and 1 in 3. Pyramids are places for spiritual initiation. Pyramids are symbol for being's inner quest. It is in the sacred confines of the Pyramids, beings would undergo the process of attaining illumination. The Great Pyramid, stood as the tallest structures, ever built – much of the recorded human history. The Great Pyramid is made up of about 2.3 million stone blocks, and all these stone blocks are being put on one foundation only. This foundation is an engineering marvel, all by itself. Sides of Pyramids are perfectly aligned with the directions on the compass. Compasses didn't actually exist back then, when Pyramids of Giza in Egypt were constructed, and also, the North Star wasn't in the same spot. Egyptian engineers would've tracked the path of stars, and then, bisected the arcs, in order to find the true North, so as to align the foundation. The Pyramids are made from Limestone, and had used the natural geology of the quarry. The thickness of each block of Limestone was determined by the thickness of the Limestone layers in the quarry. These layers would naturally separate with very little force. The great Pyramid was built in about 23 years.

CHAPTER NINE

52 Degrees 51 Minutes Concept Of Pyramid

Each side of Pyramid rises at an angle of 52 Degrees and 51 Minutes to the top. Each of the sides of the Pyramid is aligned exactly with the North, South, East, and the West. In a Pyramid, each of the four triangular-shaped sides, slope up, and converge towards each other, at the same angle, so that they meet at a point at the top, called Apex. Pyramid is constructed layer by layer, starting from the bottom. The Great Pyramid at Giza, built by Snefru's son, Khufu, also known as Cheops has its base covering over 13 Acres. Its sides rose at an angle of 52 Degrees 51 Minutes. These sides are over 755 Feet long. 52 Degrees and 51 Minutes was the angle that gave the greatest stability to the structure, while offering it a majestic look. The interior temperature of Pyramids is constant at 20 Degree Celsius, no matter, how hot it may get outside. This temperature equals the average temperature of the Earth. Meditation, when done at the centre, inside of the Pyramid shaped structure, physically and mentally energises that meditating being. Pyramid is the most stable structure on the Earth. Pyramid forms an angle 52 degrees 51 minutes, and because of this angle, pyramid receives the highest cosmic energy. This cosmic energy is maximum accumulated at King's Chamber, which is at 1/3 rd of the height of the Pyramid, from its base. However, the cosmic energy is dispersed throughout the Pyramid. Pyramid can be constructed with any material. Pyramid should be aligned perfectly with the cardinal directions, East, West, North and the South. A crystal can be fixed at the apex of the Pyramid in order to multiply the cosmic energy manifolds, and also, distribute it more uniformly throughout the Pyramid. The chosen place for the construction of Pyramid must be calm. Any size Pyramid can be constructed for the purpose of meditation at a peaceful place. Height of Pyramid should be in accordance to the base of the Pyramid. Height of a Pyramid is calculated from the formula, "Height = (Base / 1.57)". Thus, if the base is 3.14 Metres, the height of Pyramid will be 2 Metres. With the help of a Meridian Compass, which is always in the North - South direction, draw a North - South line, as the reference line to begin with. And then, aligned to this reference line, start drawing or making a square, and finally close it. This marked square will get aligned to the East, West, North, and the South cardinal directions. Also, mark the centre point, at which diagonals are intersecting, and it is the best place to meditate inside the Pyramid.

CHAPTER TEN

Meditation Inside Pyramid

Dhayana or the Meditation becomes several times easy, and also, incontrovertibly very powerful, inside a Pyramid. Cosmic energy is focussed on the being, which is doing meditation inside the Pyramid. One can easily see his or her past life during meditative state inside the Pyramid. The purpose is to influence, integrate and harmonise all levels of the being, viz. physical, mental, psychic, emotional, pranic (life force), and the spiritual. Meditation inside a Pyramid is classic instance of science meeting the nature. Pyramid has such geometry that the energy of space is converged, and also, focussed downwards. It is the reason why temples have a pyramid-shaped top. Domes also produce similar effect. Meditation improves one's integrity and the quality of consciousness. Meditation gives everything in the life. Meditation works at all the levels, viz. physical and non-physical (spiritual). Life is all about maintaining the sync among the body, mind and the spirit. Meditation is the process of establishing a conscious connection with the core or the true or the real self inside. Sleep is unconscious meditation. Meditation is a process of relaxation. In the state of relaxation, the inner space (true self), which is filled with all knowledge is, explored and experienced. Use the intuitive faculty, i.e. the gut feeling or the sixth sense for seeking answers to various problems of the life. The gut feeling is an instinct or an intuition. The gut feeling is an immediate or a basic feeling or a reaction. Yoga is a form of exercise. Yoga uses specific body postures for achieving physical and mental health benefits. Meditation is a practice, which can be done, with or without any movement. Meditation is focussing and calming the mind. Yoga is for soul, practised through the body. Yoga makes the mind quiet. Yoga finds the inner peace, and the happiness. Yoga has the ability to take the being to the present moment, where the life exists. Yoga is about self-acceptance. Yoga is the freedom from all extremes. Yoga and Meditation detoxify the body. Yoga brings a sense of balance in the ways of one's thinking, eating and living. Prayer is talking to the God. Meditation is listening to the God. Meditation liberates the being from all sufferings of the life. Enlightenment is being achieved through meditation. Meditation improves the intelligence, wisdom, and also, the understanding. Meditation strengthens willpower and the self-control. Meditation reduces the stress, and spiritually cures depression. Meditation quells irritation and anger. Meditation makes the life simply blissful. Inside or inner peace brings the outside or the outer peace. Peace is the positive state of mind. A state of "no mind" is the state of meditation. Yoga and Meditation aim at bringing elasticity to the mind. Yogasana, means a position, which is comfortable and steady. Asanas develop one's ability to sit comfortably in a position for any time duration, and it is very much needed for meditation. Raj Yoga equates Yogasana simply to the stable sitting position(s). Hatha Yoga (the Discipline of

Force) stresses mastery of the body as a way of attaining spiritual perfection, i.e. the mind being withdrawn from external objects. Hatha Yoga creates a balance between various interacting activities and processes related to the pranic and mental forces. Yoga and meditation strengthen the body, and improve the health. Beings practising Hatha Yoga (हठयोग) are called Hatha Yogis (हठयोगी). Hath Yogis have found that certain body positions open up the energy channels and the psychic centres. Hatha Yoga activates and awakens the higher centres of evolution of human consciousness. Asanas enable controlling the mind and the energies. Yogasana are the tools for achieving higher states of awareness. Yogasana provide a very stable foundation in the life, for exploring the body, the breath, the mind, and the higher states. Yogic scriptures are said to have, an original mention of 8, 400, 000 Asanas. These 8, 400, 000 Asanas represent 8.4 Million (84 Lakhs) different forms of life, based on their birth locations, called as, "84 Lakh Yonis". In the universe, infinite numbers of birth places exist, and are available for a worldly soul, for its rebirth. The groups of birth places having similar colour, odour, taste, touch and the shape, and are considered to be of one kind or one type, and the number of such birth places is 8.4 million. Every being has to pass through these 8.4 Million birth places, the evolutionary stages, before attaining liberation from the cycle of the birth and the death. Asanas represent the evolution of the life, from the simplest form to the most complex one of a fully realised human being. Through the practise of certain prescribed Asanas, the karmic processes can be sidestepped, and also, many evolutionary stages can be easily bypassed, just in one lifetime. Animals are found to live in much better harmony with, their environment, and also, their bodies. Therefore, many Yogasana are based on animal postures. Body must be supple, with steadiness and grace of movement. Prana, i.e. the vital life energy, pervades the whole body of the being. Prana has certain flow patterns, known as the Nadi. Sushumna Nadi is the central pathway of Prana, located in the spine. Yogasana and Meditation regulate and purify the Nadi. This Prana vital life energy supports the individual cellular activity. If Prana gets blocked, toxin start getting accumulated, and the body gets stiff. Flow of Prana removes the toxin accumulations from the body, thus bringing physical health to the being. Yogasana and Meditation aim at increasing the quantum of the Prana. The body must be flexible enough to take up different postures, assume various Mudras, and be able do Yogasana and Pranayama. Yogasana and Meditation awake Kundalini. Kundalini or Kundalini Shakti is the evolutionary energy. Yogasana and Meditation stimulate Chakra. Yogasana stimulating a Chakra is known as Chakrasana. Chakra is the distribution point of Kundalini Shakti within the body. Awakening Sushumna Nadi, makes Kundalini to rise up, through the spine, through all Chakras, illumining all centres of the human consciousness, up to the highest Chakra, Sahasrara. Yogasana and Meditation promote the overall health of the being, and keep his or her body in an optimum condition. Dormant energy potential is being released, and thus, confidence increases in all walks of the life. Yogasana is not the exercise, but complementary to the exercise. Exercise imposes a beneficial stress on the physical body, and thus, keeps the body ready all the time, to meet the physical demands of sudden activities. Exercises make the bones strong, and reduce the muscle waste or muscle atrophy. Exercises increase Insulin sensitivity and the capacity to absorb Oxygen. Yogasana is a technique of stretching or massaging or placing the physical body in Mudras, postures and the positions, which cultivates relaxation, meditation, awareness and the concentration, by stimulating the Pranic channels and the internal organs. Contrary to the exercises, Yogasana when performed, arrests catabolism (destructive metabolism), slows down the rates of respiration and the metabolism, leading to the drop of, the body temperature and the absorption levels of the Oxygen. Yogasana and Meditation alter electrochemical activity of the nervous system. Yogasana and Meditation, i.e. Meditation Asanas have special effects on glands and internal organs. Meditation is the higher state of Yoga. Always breathe through the nose. During meditation, be continuously aware, i.e. consciously note, thoughts and feeling, the sensations of the body, posture of the body, any physical movement of the body, breath patterns, movement of Prana, and concentrate on Chakras. Relaxation must be practised at the end. Sequence is important. Counterpoise through counter pose is quite necessary to bring the body back to the balanced normal state. What is being done to the Left, should also be done to the Right, and the vice versa. Yogasana and Meditation can be done any time except after the meals. However, the time before the Sunrise is "the best". In the evening, time around the Sunset is also a favourable time. Yogasana and Meditation can be done by the beings of any age, and the gender. Outdoors is the best place of practising Yogasana and Meditation. However, a well-ventilated room in the house is also a good option. Practising Yogasana and Meditation inside the Pyramid, is "the best option". Use a natural blanket to sit on, while practicing Yogasana and Meditation. Also, this blanket will act as an insulator between the body and the Earth. Wear loose, light coloured and comfortable clothes. Empty the bowels and take a cold shower before starting. Stomach should be empty at the time of practise. Later, eat natural food, in moderation. During practise, there should be no unnecessary straining, and stop immediately, if some contraindications are being observed. Inverted postures must be practised with care and prudence. If one meditates inside the pyramid, "the no thought state", also known as, "Nirmala Sthithi" is being attained three to four times faster as otherwise. Pyramid facilitates very easy communication with the higher frequencies. Meditation inside the Pyramid has healing effect, and also, there are other paranormal experiences. Chant "AUM". Word AUM is just not a word, but a power, which contains all the vibrations of the universe. Meditation protects a being from the dark energies. Brain contains billions of neurons. Electrical impulse of various frequencies, travel through neurons of neural network inside the brain. A Brainwave is an electrical impulse in the brain. Brainwaves are of five types, categorised on the basis of frequency of oscillations of their electrical impulses. In the increasing order of their frequencies of oscillations, and the decreasing order of their amplitudes, these five Brainwaves are, the Delta, the Theta, the Alpha, the Beta, and the Gamma. Simultaneously, all Brainwaves are present in the brain, but at a time, depending upon the kind of activity done, only one Brainwave dominates over the others. Frequency Range of Delta Brainwave is 0.1 - 3.5 Hz.. During sleep, in the dreamless state, this Delta Brainwave becomes predominant. This Delta Brainwave produces healing effects. Up to the age of one year, these Delta Brainwave is dominant in infants. Delta Brainwave accesses the data and the information stored in the Unconscious

Mind, and being moves away from physical nature of the life. Frequency Range of the Theta Brainwave is 4 - 8 Hz.. Sensations, emotions and memories are carried in the Theta Brainwave. Theta Brainwave exists between the sleep state and wakeful state. Theta Brainwave accesses the data and the information stored in the Subconscious Mind. In the dream state during the sleep, or during daydreaming, or during deep meditation, or during deep rest state of the mind, this Theta Brainwave becomes dominant. Theta Brainwave also occurs during the states of insightfulness and lower consciousness. Theta Brainwave is dominant during the tasks, which do not need attention. Frequency Range of Alpha Brainwave is 1 - 12 Hz.. Alpha Brainwave is dominant during, creative tasks, Yoga, and in, closed eye state, calm and conscious states, and also, mentally and physically relaxed states. Alpha Brainwave acts as a bridge between the Conscious Mind and the Subconscious Mind. Frequency Range of Beta Brainwave is 13 - 32 Hz.. Beta Brainwave is dominant during Active Thinking. Active Thinking is the practice of translating ideas or thoughts into actions leading to meaningful innovations and solutions. Beta Brainwave is also dominant during fully alert and awakened brain state like during active conversation, problem solving and the decision making. Frequency Range of Gamma Brainwave is 32 - 40 Hz.. When the brain is used to its full capacity like during heavy data and information processing, and deep problem solving and serious calculations, Gamma Brainwave becomes dominant. Meditation is an activity, which eventually makes the being to experience the universe, and its powers, and the God, provided he or she does not get cold feet during the meditation process. The poses of Meditation, i.e. the Asanas, are in the shape of Pyramids. Siddhasana, the seated Asana, assumes a Triangular shape, i.e. the shape of Pyramid. Spirituality is about moving from compulsiveness to the consciousness. One word to characterise the Meditation and the Yoga, is "supercalifragilisticexpialidocious".

CHAPTER ELEVEN

Astral Travel And Time Travel

Astral Travel is a Siddhi. Siddhi is a paranormal power possessed by a Siddha. Siddha is a being, which has attained a Siddhi. Siddhi happens through various practices like Meditation, Pranayama (Breathing exercises), Mantra chanting and the Asana. Asana is a Sanskrit word. Asana means, "a posture", or "a seat", or simply "a place". Astral Travel is also known as Astral Projection. Astral Travel is an Out – of - Body Experience (OBE). There exists subtle body, known as the "Astral Body". Astral Body is capable of travelling through the Astral Planes. Through the Astral Body, being's consciousness can function separately from his or her physical body. In Astral Travel, subtle body (consciousness) is being separated from the physical body. Astral Travel happens in Near – Death - Experience (NDE). Also, Astral Travel can happen due to one's conscious efforts for it. Thus, in the Astral Travel, physical body, mental body, energy body and the bliss body are left intact. In Astral Travel, only the etheric body floats around. There is a definite Astral World, which can be very easily traversed during the meditation. Dream Yoga, awakens the consciousness in the inner worlds, and facilitates Astral

Travel through the process of lucid dreaming. Inner World means everything that one can experience inside of him or her. Inner World is everything, which is hidden from the outside view. Inner World includes, thoughts, self - talks, images flashing in the eyes of the mind etc.. In, lucid dreaming, the dreamer becomes aware, what he or she is dreaming about, while the dreaming. In lucid dreaming, the dreamer has control over, the dream characters, narrative, and the environment. While in Astral Travel, a being can still the physical activities as the physical body, the mental body and the energy body are intact. Body is made up of three bodies, viz. the physical, the astral, and the causal. Within these three bodies, there are five Koshas or sheaths. These five Koshas or sheaths are, the physical body (Annamaya Kosha), the energy body (Pranamaya Kosha), the mental body (Manomaya Kosha), the wisdom body (Vijnanamaya Kosha), and the bliss body (Anandamaya Kosha). Physical body, mental body and energy body are physical, whereas bliss body is totally beyond the physical. The etheric body or the ether - body or simply the aether body, is the subtle body. Etheric body is the first or the lowest layer in the human energy field or the aura. Etheric body is the immediate contact with the physical body. Etheric body sustains the physical body, and also, connects the physical body with the higher bodies. "Etheric" is a transitory energy. It is neither physical nor beyond. It is simply a transition. Etheric body is sensed in a certain state or a certain level of the Sadhana (spiritual practices or disciplines), and the intensity within.

Time Travel is the travel, through the times, into the past or the future. Beings are always travelling though times, from the past into the present, and then into the future. Time is different for different realms or dimensions.

In Time Travel, being's mind and the body remain unchanged, with his or her memories intact, while his or her location in time is changed. Wormhole is a feature of space - time, which provides a short - cut through the time and the space. In the Quantum Physics, the proven concepts like Superposition, Entanglement etc., mean that a particle can be in two or even more places at once. Quantum Time presents a view of "many worlds". Many worlds simply mean that different quantum states exist simultaneously, in multiple parallel universes, within an overall multiverse. Time Travel takes place, when access is gained to these alternative parallel universes. The equations of relativity imply that faster – than - light particles, also known as the Superluminal Particles, e.g. Tachyons, would travel backwards in the time. For a Tachyon, the speed of light is the lower speed limit. Tachyon's upper speed limit is infinity. Tachyon's speed increases as its energy decreases. In meditation, both, viz. the Astral Travel, and the Time Travel, occur at a later stage.

Meet the real self, and also, the ideal self, through Astral Travel, Time Travel, Yoga, and Meditation inside the Pyramid; Retrouvaille. Astral Travel, Time Travel, Yoga, and Meditation inside the Pyramid improve balance and proprioception.

CHAPTER TWELVE

Multiverse

There are many parallel universes, known as the multiverse. Interestingly, each one of us has five more versions of us, which exist simultaneously in other parallel universes. The multiverse is a space or a realm, which consists of a number of universes. Our universe is one of these universes. These other universes are like our universe only. These parallel universes have their own, galaxies, blackholes and civilisations. Blackhole is a region of space with quite intense gravitational field, from which no matter or radiation can escape. These parallel universes have their own planets, like this universe. Every universe has hyperspace structure, and has multiple dimensions. Ten dimensions are Length, Breadth, Height or Depth, Time, Possibility, Alternates (which creates stories, as each universe is made up of different destinies, which results in varied consequences across various dimensions, i.e. the karma of the universe), Infinities (creating continuum), Ubiquity, Law, and the Demiurge (the Creator). Universe is a reflection of the divine perfection. There is a greater power at work always, which guides and shapes the lives in many ways, which are simply beyond comprehension. The universe is a vast mysterious place. Universe is impenetrable and inscrutable. Universe is just another name for an existing higher power, having its different names, viz. the God, or the Source, or the Consciousness. Universe is a high vibrational energy boundless space. The universe is all - knowing, all - powerful, and all - present. Universe is a very vast interconnected web of energy, which connects everything, and also, everyone, within it. Trying to connect with the universe is trying to connect with the higher self. Also, it is getting connected to the divine source of all creation. Higher self means an eternal, omnipotent, conscious, and the intelligent ideal being. Connection with the universe, simply brings, love, peace, love, understanding, and the harmony. Through Meditation, a being can very easily connect him or herself to the universe(s). We all are parts of something much bigger than ourselves. We all are all connected to one another. Also, we are connected to the greater cosmic order all the time. This connection gives meaning to the life, and creates an understanding to treat others with full compassion and all respect. Meditation helps the beings finding their purpose of the life. In order to connect with the universe, do meditation, which quietens the mind, and opens the heart. Meditate on the nature of the universe. Spend time in the nature. Sharing is caring. It is the universe, which creates the life and all its effects. All manifestations are handiworks of the universe. Corresponding to the vibrational frequency of every being, the universe responds, and sends such other beings into his or her life. Situations and the experiences are created by the universe for a being in accordance with the vibrational frequency of that being. Positive vibrations bring positive results, and negative vibrations bring negative results in the life. Results are created by the universe for us, according to our thoughts, and the actions. The universe acknowledges and respects every thought and action of being. We are one with the cosmos. Everything done, affects us, everyone, and everything else, in the universe. Everything is energy, and the energy travels. We are energy. Thought is energy. Action is energy. Also, the energy cannot be destroyed by any means. Energy can only be transformed. Understand the interconnectedness of everything. Live the life with compassion, and the awareness. Everything that happens is simply an opportunity to grow, and to evolve. Universe has created us. Universe can never do anything, which is bad for us. Universe simply wants us to grow, and to make spiritual progress, as our real spiritual parents. Universe is parent of all parents. Universe has nothing to do with our physical progress, growth and accumulations. What is of the universe, and also real, goes with us, after the death. And, what is unreal, stays back on the earth after the death, and we are gone without it. We all are trapped in the play of the universe. However, the universe wishes to teach and enlighten us all the time.

CHAPTER THIRTEEN

Need Of A Permanent Living Master

Everything in its state of impermanence exists in this permanent Multiverse. Fixity of the God is the only truth, as creation's existence also proves creator's existence. We all must establish ourselves in our ideal self, in our own right, in our own accord. Ideal self is the kind of the being, you want to become. While on the spiritual path in the journey of life, there is need of a Permanent Living Master (PLM), or a Spiritual Guru. Permanent Living Master shows the right path. Permanent Living Master guides us at every moment of the life. It is the grace of the Permanent Living Master in the life, which brings peace, happiness, joy, celebration, fearlessness and exuberance in the life. Without a Permanent Living Master, it is not possible to move the energy from Third Eye Chakra to Crown Chakra (Sahasrara). The Crown Chakra is the highest Chakra, which comes after the other six Chakras, viz. Root Chakra, Sacral Chakra, Solar Plexus Chakra, Heart Chakra, Throat Chakra, and the Third Eye Chakra. Chakras make up the subtle energy system of the body. Sahasrara is the connection point of the human life force, within the body with the universe or the existence. The Crown Chakra is the individual's center of the spirit, the enlightenment, the wisdom, the universal consciousness, and connection to the higher guidance. Crown Chakra is the highest potential. The Crown Chakra governs interaction and communication with the universe. The Crown Chakra signifies one's senses of inspiration and devotion, the union with the higher self and the divinity, and a deeper understanding. The Crown Chakra is responsible for a healthy spiritual life. The Crown Chakra is not on the body, but a little away from the body on the top. One has to jump in order to reach this Crown Chakra or needs a tight hand-holding by the Permanent Living Master. The Crown Chakra is the state of complete enlightenment and sheer bliss. Whirlpool Vortex or the Bhanwar Gupha or the Hootal Hoot located between Third Eye Chakra and the Crown Chakra is a rotating swing tunnel, which is very specifically related to the Chakras. This tunnel is always in a subtle motion, and the spirit ever swings on it. As experienced, there are innumerable spiritual islands in this tunnel, at its near end, from which the sounds "Sohang Sohang" and "Ana-Hoo Ana-Hoo" rise all the time. Spirit playfully and rapturously enjoys these sounds. There are whiffs of scents of various sorts, and sweet fragrance of sandal is spread all-over, which is greatly enjoyed by the spirit, while it proceeds onwards. Also, melodies of flutes are heard. It is the Permanent Living Master or the Guru, which pulls a being's soul or the spirit through this tunnel, onto the other side of it, as otherwise, it is generally not possible for a being to pass the tunnel on his or her own spiritual efforts, after his or her physical death, and thus, spirit is being returned back to the physical plane again, i.e. the earth, at least for one more birth and journey of life. A soul or the spirit has no gender. Heaven or Sach Khand is there on the other side of this tunnel.

The soul or the spirit has to ascend up to the Sach Khand, while successfully passing through this tunnel. Garden of Eden or the Garden of Bliss is in the heaven. Garden of Eden is the paradise created by the God himself to inhabit first human creation, viz. the Adam and the Eve. Garden of Eden is a very sacred place. There are sacred trees in the Garden of Eden, like the Tree of the Knowledge of Good and Evil, Tree of Life etc.. It is the region of healing and divine lights and sounds. Ascension of the soul is facilitated by the Permanent Living Master or the Spiritual Guru. Do Meditation inside the Pyramid under the guidance of a Permanent Living Master.

CHAPTER FOURTEEN

Ancient Wisdom

Being, which avoids failure, also avoids the success. Love, and enjoy, every moment of life. Do not try saving the moments, as there is no system to get a refund on the unused moments of the life. Stop expecting others to make you happy. The basic nature of being's consciousness is the consciousness of lacking the things in the given physical life. Wisdom is making good judgements. The ability to make good judgements is based on learning from the past experiences, the knowledge, and the understanding. Ancient wisdom provides insight and practical answers to social, economic, and personal problems. Yoga, Meditation, Worship, Yantra, Mantra, Tantra, Religious Text etc., are the elements of ancient wisdom. Tantra uses Yantra and Mantra in order to reach up to the universe for guidance, help and support. Wisdom provides means to communicate with the universe, and to access the God. Ancient wisdom helps in living a more fulfilled and meaningful life. Ancient wisdom has the power to change the life. Listen with intent, as listening is the key to understanding. Study own failings; it helps develop the right understanding and the right perspective. Look within the self, before pointing at the others. One's reaction(s) to the situations changes the whole narrative. Do not fear the change. Do not get stuck in the ways. Embrace the change to enjoy the life. It is called adaptation. Always put the opinion(s) in most accurate context in order to win the conversation. Think right. Act right. There is always an opportunity in the midst of the chaos. There is always a hope in the uncertainty. Develop a good strong character; it is an organic process. Happiness depends on the quality of the thoughts. Keep changing the tracks, if needed, in order to be successful. Always, remain in the learning mode. Positively impact the lives of others. Choose to love others, and not to hate the others. Leave back a rich legacy of yours, before you are gone. We are gods. We should keep pushing and expanding our horizons; keep changing the surroundings. This full universe is ours. We must place our worth on our values, and not on the wealth. Money cannot buy happiness. Money cannot buy wisdom. Manage the mind. Control the mind. Have a sound mind. If mind is being controlled, events get controlled. Mind is unlimited. Be kind to every being, and to everything. Kindness is the power. Love is the biggest power. Kindness and love are positive energies. Kindness creates love. Love is the basis of whole creation. Value the relations and the relationships. Conquer the self. Life is a big responsibility. Life in the real sense is created by us, and quality to it, is added by us. Work on the life. Life is the greatest masterpiece. Do not corrupt the thought process. Do not judge or blame others. No being is perfect here. Build a resilient future. Accept beings as they are, but place them in the life, as you like. In the modern times, ancient wisdom has a much greater role to play in shaping the lives of beings and the state of the planet, and thus, creating a far beautiful and peaceful world full of harmony, peace, happiness and love. Vedanta is the guide for life in today's times. Vedanta is search for self - knowledge, and also, a search for the God. Vedanta affirms oneness of the whole existence, divinity of the soul, and the understanding and harmony among all world religions. Divinity is our real nature. Identify the self with everything, and not with something, or just with few things. Take a leap of faith in harder times or trying situations. Vedanta teaches about four paths to achieve the goal of understanding divine nature of self, viz. Bhakti Yoga (prayer, chanting, and meditation on the God), Jnana Yoga (reasoning and discernment), Karma Yoga (detachment and equanimity in work), and Raja Yoga (meditation). Bhakti Yoga is the path of love and devotion. Jnana Yoga is the path of knowledge. Karma Yoga is the path of selfless work. Karma Yoga teaches that results of actions are beyond our control. Raja Yoga is the path of Meditation. Meditation makes us to experience higher states of the consciousness. Meditation makes us to achieve a deeper understanding of our divine nature. Mantra based Meditation technique uses symbolic images of the divine. Learn to be calm by anyways, the nature's ways, using various techniques, as prescribed in the Ancient Wisdom.

CHAPTER FIFTEEN

Frequency, Vibrations And Energy

We all get our comeuppance; it is the Law of Universe. Life has some bigger purpose. God is with us always, around us, in some form, some body's form, to boost us, to encourage us, to assist us, and takes us through the dark forests of the journey of life, onto the other side of it, where there is light, peace, joy, love, and the happiness. Journey of life is a roller coaster ride. Avoid becoming meat in the sandwich. Moving on the path of spirituality must be every being's swan-song, if not done sooner in the life. Thought is the power. Thought creates the action. Thought is frequency, vibration and the energy. We all are vibrations. Everything in the life is a vibration. Universe is a vibration. God is also a vibration. Vibration has certain frequency. Higher is the frequency, higher will be the vibrations. Everything is vibration in the life. Things are being controlled by the vibrations. Every particle, molecule and atom vibrates. It is an ever expanding universe. There is no beginning, and no end to it. It is simply beyond comprehension. Change is the only constant here. Principle of Uncertainty is only existing certainty here in this entire creation. Vibrations define and characterise mass or the matter or the material, and the energy. Things here in the cosmos, have different vibrational levels. Therefore, things have different frequencies. Universe and its things and events can only be comprehended in terms of levels of, frequency, vibrations and the energy. Universe vibrates at the frequency of 432 Hz.. The planet earth vibrates at a natural frequency of 7.83 Hz.. Thus, there is a repeating atmospheric heartbeat, i.e. vibrations of earth, like our heartbeat. This atmospheric heartbeat, encircles the earth, and is strongly present between the earth's surface and a boundary about 60 miles upon the earth, known as the "Schumann Resonance". This natural frequency of the earth protects all on the earth. Frequencies change the feelings, mood and the emotions. Frequencies affect the physical, the mental, and the emotional health of beings. Presence of low frequencies around 19 Hz. or even less, develops fear and anxiety in beings. Human beings can listen the sound of frequencies in the range of 20 to 20 kHz.. A being feels relaxed, and becomes quite happy, peaceful and calm in the presence of frequency of 432 Hz.. "Energy in motion", is emotion. Good emotions are related to higher frequency or higher vibrations or the higher energy, and the bad emotions are related to lower frequency or lower vibrations or the lower energy. The frequency of 432 Hz. has healing effects on the mind, body, and the spirit. Meditation is the process of establishing self in the state of resonance with the frequency of the earth, and the other frequencies of the universe. Human beings have frequency of 7.5 Hz.. Enlightenment occurs at a frequency of 700 Hz., and beyond 700 Hz., mind enters into a blissful state of self-realisation with no ego, which is known as the "Superconsciousness". "Superconsciousness" is beyond the states of consciousness and the subconscious. Peace is above the emotions of joy and love, and is found at 600 Hz. Similarly, others emotions are created at certain other frequencies, e.g. joy at 540 Hz. love at 500 Hz., acceptance at 350 Hz., neutrality (neutral state) at 250 Hz., courage at 200 Hz., pride at 175 Hz., anger at 150 Hz., desire at 125 Hz., grief at 75 Hz., guilt at 30 Hz., and shame at 20 Hz.. Desire is the basis for many bad and evil emotions. Live the life in a state of detached attachments. Mental state is a vibration. Strength of a being is, when he or she has so much to cry for, but he or she prefers to smile instead. Happiness is not about getting the things, but all about, enjoying the things already one has. Being's health is his or her greatest gift. Contentment is the greatest wealth. And, being faithful is the best relationship. When a being desires a thing so deeply that he or she is willing to stake his or her entire future on a single turn of the wheel in order to get that thing, he or she will surely get that thing in his or her life. Universe helps being in his or her strong unshakable commitments and resolutions, and endeavours. Problems will come in the life, as they are the part of life, and facing these problems is the art of life. Life is designed with problems, pains and pleasures. Words spoken, is the confession of one's own character. What is heard, is one's opinion, and not the fact. Similarly, what is seen, is one's perspective, and not the truth. We all are vibrational energies with certain frequencies.

CHAPTER SIXTEEN

Breath Control

Breathing Technique is an entry - level easy Meditation. Breath Control is also known as the Breath Meditation. Focus attention on the breath; it reduces stress, and brings immediate relaxation. Breath Control quells errant Stress Response. Stress Response is also known as, "Fight or Flight". Stress Response is body's preparation to confront and avert the imminent lurking danger. Stress Breath Control protects the health. Breathing Meditation requires a comfortable position in a silent place with minimum distractions. One may sit down, or stand, or even walk. Sitting position is best for Breath Control. During the Breath Control, have a sustained focus on the mind, such as, repetition of a sound or a word or a phrase or a movement. Further, allow thoughts to come and go away, while focusing on repetition. Breathe - in slowly through the nose, allowing the chest and lower belly to rise, as lungs are getting filled with the air. Let the abdomen expand fully. Retain air there for some comfortable time duration, and then, breathe out slowly through the mouth. Focus on the breath. Regularly practice this controlled breathing. While doing it, sit comfortably with eyes closed. Blend deep breathing with helpful imagery or a focus word or a phrase, which helps to relax. Focus full attention on breathing. Feel breath's natural rhythm, and its flow, and also the way, breath feels on each inhale and exhale. Focusing on the breath turns attention away, and brings calm and peace during stress or negative emotions. Observing the breath simply opens the doors of a healthy and mindful life. Always, have a restful sleep. Mindful breathing through breath control is a very powerful mindfulness meditation practice. Psychological stress has detrimental, deleterious and devastating effects on being's health. Health is not only physical, but also, mental and emotional. Stress is associated with anxiety, depression, high blood pressure, heart diseases, cancer, poor memory, several aches and pains. Breath Meditation relieves stress. Breath Meditation leads to practice of "mindfulness". In mindfulness, one learns to accept and appreciate, what comes in his or her way of life. Also, in the mindfulness, one stops fighting with his or her own thoughts and feelings. Breathe deeply through the nose, while fully filling the lungs. In Deep Breathing, lower belly rises. Deep Breathing is also known as Diaphragmatic Breathing or Abdominal Breathing or Belly Breathing or Paced Respiration. Do not hold in stomach muscles, as it interferes with the Deep Breathing, and leads to shallow Chest Breathing, which increases tension and anxiety. Shallow Chest Breathing limits lung diaphragm's range of motion, as a result, the lower part of lungs don't its due share of oxygenated air, and one feels short of breath. Deep abdominal breathing leads to full oxygen exchange, lowering the heartbeat rate, and stabilising the Blood Pressure. Other relaxation techniques are Yoga, Progressive Muscle Relaxation, Guided Imagery, Mindfulness Meditation, Tai Chi, Qi Gong, Repetitive Prayer, etc.. Breath Control helps to achieve soundness of the mind. Deep

Breathing relieves stress and frustration. Breath Control is the foundation of Stress Management. A good breath work is a Deep Diaphragmatic Breathing (Belly Breathing or Breathing Rehabilitation), which triggers relaxation responses in the body by enhancing physical, spiritual, and mental, health and wellness. Breath work is a mind - body therapy, which includes several breathing practices like Yogic Breathing, Clarity Breath Work, Holotropic Breathing etc.. Breath work alleviates Post - Traumatic Stress Disorder (PTSD) and improves immune response. Breath Control mitigates Asthma. Breath Control aids in Chronic Obstructive Pulmonary Disease (COPD) rehabilitation. Also, Breath Control aids Glycemic control in beings having Type-2 Diabetes. Glycemic Index (GI) is a measure of how quickly food makes the blood sugar, i.e. the Glucose, to rise. Foods containing Carbohydrates have GI. Breath Control improves the quality of life, in general of all the beings, and in particular, of those beings, which have cardiovascular disease(s) and / or cancer. Breath work reduces anxiety, and the depression. Breath work, sharpens the memory, promotes better restful sleep, and improves heart's health.

CHAPTER SEVENTEEN

Power Of Aum

Aum (Om or ओउम् or ॐ) is a "mantra", and not any symbol. Aum is the sound of the universe. Aum sound is the "hum" sound of the earth. Mantra is a word or a prayer, which is chanted or sung. Aum is the sacred sound of the universe. Aum encompasses all other sounds within it. Aum represents the three deities, the Brahma (A), the Vishnu (U), and the Mahesh (M) or the Shiva. Brahma is the Creator. Vishnu is the Preserver or Sustainer. Mahesh or Shiva is the Destroyer. Aum mantra helps in transacting the mind. Aum mantra comprises three sounds of 'A', 'U' and 'M'. Aum is a means to unite all those, anything and everything, which is around us. Aum represents the beginning, i.e. creation of the universe ("A"- an elongated awe), the middle ("U" - a prolonged sound "oooh"), and also, the end ("M" - sound "mmmm"). Thus, "Aum" represents everything of this infinite creation and the existence. Aum represents the past, the present, and also, the future. "A" signifies conscious or wakeful state, the openness. "U" signifies dream state, the steadiness, the preserving energy, which sustains everything. And, "M" signifies the state of deep sleep, the closing, the finalisation, or the beginning of end, the culmination, the completion.

Sound of "A" originates in the belly. Sound of "A" vibrates the upper chest. Sound of "U" makes the lips to move together. Sound of "U" then from the lips gradually moves forward, which rolls along the upper palate. Sound of "U" creates vibrations in the throat. Sound of "M" is formed by moving the tongue towards the top of the mouth, and then, bring the lips together, in order to create a protracted humming, the sound "mmmm". Utternace of "Aum" with purity, connects the being to the underlying consciousness, i.e. the "Atman" or the soul, the underlying reality. Aum is the sound of unification. Aum is the sound, utterance of which, brings the peace, happiness, contentment and fulfillment in the life, and brings the Atman (the soul) close, to get connected to the Parmatman (the God). Aum carries the concepts of the life and the death. Aum connects the beings with the divinity reality. Aum chanting is a very powerful meditation. Sound and vibrations existed at the time of the creation of this cosmos. Aum creates sound, energy and the vibrations of the universe. Uttering "Aum" is resonating the self with the universe. In the state of resonance of self with the universe, the true self gets purified. Live and lead the life of detachment such that nothing owns you. Other's judgements and opinions do not define one's reality, and the personality. Make the life, while busy making the living, as otherwise, life comes back to square one, meaning again, another birth after the death, i.e. the rebirth.

CHAPTER EIGHTEEN

The Sound Of Silence

Along with three sounds of the mantra Aum, the fourth sound of the universe or the creation is the sound of the silence. Aum consists of four syllables, viz. A, U, M, and the silent syllable. The sound of silence is the residue or the energy, which we are left with, once the breath and all other sounds fade away. The sound of silence arises from the stillness. The sound of silence is maintained by the steadiness. And finally, the sound of silence again fades back into the silence. Silence is beautiful. Silence is the bliss. Silence is peace. Silence is powerful. Sound of silence teaches the loudest lessons of the life. Sound of life is the divine silence. The sound of silence helps one to experience the emptiness, the selflessness, uncertainties, and the transient nature of all experiences of the life, and also, the patterns of the consciousness. Meditation is the journey from movement to the stillness. The practise of listening to the sound of silence develops one's attention, and maintains his or her continuity of mindfulness. When mind becomes calm and focussed, the breath becomes quiet and quieter. Mantra Aum (Om or ओउम् or ॐ) represents the very truth or the fact that everything in the universe or the creation is constantly changing, changing from the movement into the stillness, changing from the sound into the silence; as it is the endless cycle of the show of life and the creation of the God. Doing what one likes is the freedom of life, and liking what one does is the happiness of life. Do inner sound meditation. Sharpen the faculty of intuition, which helps in listening to the inner sound. Inner sound is the esoteric essence of the God, which is available to all beings. Sound Meditation uses the sound for cultivating and supporting deep relaxation. Sound Meditation creates a gentle powerful experience, which heals the body, declutters the mind, and reins the attention in the present. Nada Yoga is the practice of deep internal listening, i.e. hearing the sound of Anahata Nada. Anahata Nada is one's own inner unstruck sound, which otherwise is inaccessible to the others. The Nada Sound or the Nada Vibration is produced, when we hit on a Sound Bowl or a Gong. Anahata Nada sound is similar to the beating of the waves of the sea or the peals of huge bells or the holy sound of conch. Every sound has its medium, and produces vibrations. Every sound has its definite source. Silence is the stillness of the mind. Silence brings forth the truth of everything. Silence is never empty, but always replete with answers to all the questions of the life. Meditation is the journey from sound to the silence. Listening to the sound of silence takes one from his or her limited identity to the unlimited infinite space. Sound of silence is the happiness. All wise souls speak very loudly in the silence. Silence nourishes the wisdom. The act of creation is always silent, as a seed sprouts in the silence. Soil silently adds to the growth of a sapling to grow into a big tree one day. Nature works in silence. Construction is always silent. Destruction may be devoid of the silence. Life begins and thrives in the silence. Silence is greatest art of loudest and most effective conversation, as silence is always wiser than a speech. Emotions travel through the medium of silence. Silence is the total harmony. Inner sound meditation develops, better understanding, increased concentration and observation and perception, increased energy, and increased love and compassion. Sound of silence is everywhere. Sound of silence never changes. Sound of silence is present, both internally, and also, externally. Birth and death both, happen in the silence. Sound of silence is the biggest secret of this God's creation. Sound is temporary, but silence is permanent. Every sound begins from the sound and ends in the silence. Thus, silence is the both, the source or the beginning as well as the end of sound. Silence is ultimate truth of the life. All beings need silence in their lives, as it is their basic nature and the need. Silence only brings lasting peace and the happiness in the lives of beings. Sound of silence is the voice of the spirit or the soul inside, and also, of the universe outside. Interestingly, inside is the outside and outside is the inside. Listening to the sound of the silence is, connecting with the soul, i.e. the true self, a journey to the emptiness (the Shiva). The sound of silence is the permanent companion of every being, whether he or she is alone or not. Listening to the sound of silence makes one to live in the present, and get the most out of the moments of the journey of life. Sound is like a wave in the ocean of silence.

CHAPTER NINETEEN

Prayer

Prayer is powerful. Life is too fragile; handle it well, by using the powers of prayer. Life is made beautiful through prayers, sacrifices, humility and love. Feel the love of giving. Life without prayer is a life without input of power. Prayer is longing of the soul. Prayer aligns the being with the wishes of the God. God is the most silent aspect of the life. Prayer creates a connection with the God. God cannot be put in any kind of format. Accept the God as the wind and as a presence. God is the presence. When a being becomes presence, he or she becomes everything. Feel the size of the God. Prayer is putting the self in the hands of the God. This whole creation is the God. Perceive the grandeur of consciousness of the God through prayer. God is at every place. Through prayers, it is possible to listen to the voice of the God, deep in the depths of the heart. Normal beings operate from two levels of the intelligence, viz. the intelligence to process the acquired knowledge, and the logical intelligence. Acquired knowledge is gained externally from the environment, whereas, the logical intelligence is the truth created by the self through introspection, analyses etc.. Truth is always transformative; it transforms the being. Truth is permanent in nature. Truth is never an imagination or a hallucination, which is too ephemeral and temporary in nature. Truth stabilises the being. Truth enlightens the being. However, there is another level, the third level, which is known as cosmic consciousness (Ritambhara Buddhi). Ritambhara is a certain meditative frequency, which destroys all illusion tendencies of mind. Masters operate at this third level, i.e. the level of cosmic consciousness. This third level can only be achieved after achieving the first and the second levels. Cosmic consciousness is complete perpetual awareness. There are three states within the state of cosmic consciousness, viz. Wakeful state (the state of communication and connections with the external or outside world using organs of perceptions and organs of actions; experiencing the positions, the possessions, and the relations), Dream state (the state of processing the received and stored data acquired in the Wakeful state, e.g. seeing what is looked or listening what is heard; mind, intellect and ego process the data), and the Deep Sleep state. These three states are three states of the spirit in 24 hours. When these three states dilute within themselves, being reaches the fourth state in the state of the cosmic consciousness, known as the Turiya state. The Turiya state is the state of pure total awareness, with no ownership or doership (the state of being a doer) of actions, and only responding. Response comes to every earnest prayer, thus brings gratification and completeness to being performing such a prayer. God is the presence. Prayer is imploring the heavenly interference. In the state of cosmic consciousness, there is no death. All gods are still present and will always remain present, as beings remember them. Remembrance creates the connection. Consciousness is huge and dimensionless. Consciousness is infinite in size. Consciousness is unknowable and unfathomable. All incarnations of God and masters are still there. Their consciousness is right next to every being. In the state of prayer, remember the God, feel the presence of the God. In the state of prayer, feel that you are an existing element of God's creation, the child of the God. Feel that, the presence here, is due to the will of the God. If the God did not want, I would not have been here. Experience the God. God takes full care of beings responsibilities without saying. Do not worry in the life. Surrender to the God in the prayer. Prayer is the best medicine. Manage the mind. Mind creates thoughts. Thoughts emerge from desires, tendencies, inclinations and the impressions of the past. Meditation is listening to the God. In the prayer, focus on the God. Feel that, you are performing prayer for the God. Faith and prayer are invisible. Prayer is talking to the God. Feel in the prayer that you are the God. God always delivers. God's help is only a prayer away, have unshakeable and unfathomable faith in the God, and in the powers of the universe. We all are born here with certain purpose. We all are the responsibility of the nature, the existence, and the God. Pray to the God for his consciousness. Pray to the God to experience his huge, cosmic, multidimensional consciousness and the God will deliver it, for God is the consciousness. Never pray for small things, but always for big and permanent things. Faith and prayer make the impossible, possible. Miracles do happen. God is everything in this existence. Perform the prayer with an open heart and an open mind. Perform the prayer in the state of full surrender to the God. God is the supreme consciousness. God is the power of prayer. God always gives more than expectation and the imagination, in his own ways, in his own time and space. Touching the feet, is touching the consciousness. Feet represent the stability. Masters are established in the state of cosmic consciousness. Masters are established in the stable state of awareness of consciousness. Beings are representations of the consciousness, but grossly deluded due to the false identifications. We beings, in reality, are the supreme consciousness. Go empty for prayer. Purify the soul through the prayers. All experiences of the life are the experiences of the spirit, which affect the soul. Soul does not experience anything. Soul is the source, and also the end. Soul is the silence, and spirit is the sound. The operational element of the soul is the spirit. Soul and the spirit are different, and not the same. Spirit has the ability to move and get activated. God operates through the soul within all of us. Become silent and happy by performing the prayer. Thinking or a chattering mind cannot listen, therefore silent the mind. Spirit through the body, experiences the life, for soul's evolution. Remember, that no one can make feel inferior unhappy without self-consent. When the life changes to be hard, change yourself to be strong. Prayer changes us, and then, we change the things, situations and the circumstances as confronted in the journey of life. Prayer is always invigorating. God's infinite grace and power is bestowed on us, when we pray. Make prayer a habit. Know your provenance. Being's hope is concerned with the eschatology, i.e. the science of last things.

CHAPTER TWENTY

Pranayama

Pranayama is the main component of Yoga. Pranayama is one of the eight limbs of Yoga. Pranayama is intended to expand Prana (the life energy or life force). Prana is the universal energy, which flows in form of currents, in and around the body. Pranayama is the Yogic Practice of focussing on breath. Breath is the life – giving force. Shiva, also known as the Adiyogi, is the god of Yoga. Adiyogi is patron god of yoga, meditation and the arts. Pranayama is a Sanskrit language word. In the language Sanskrit, word "Prana" means the life energy, and the word "Ayama" means control. Thus, Pranayama is the control of life energies. Pranayama is a means to elevate the Prana Shakti or the life energies. Prana is restricted from flowing through Sushumna by the locks, which remain above each chakra. These locks primarily function to stop the activation and flow of Kundalini from entering the Sushumna, and then, rising up to the Crown Chakra. Sushumna or Sushumna Nadi is the main energy channel of the subtle body. Kundalini is the latent female energy, which is lying coiled at the base of the spine. Crown Chakra or Sahasrara is seventh primary chakra located at the top of the head. Chakra means energy centre. Crown Chakra relates with the spiritual connection and the transformation. Crown Chakra lifts and inspires the being, and connects him or her to the divine. Pranayama is also known by the words, Breathwork, or Asana, or Orujjayi, or Qi-gong, or Null. Pranayama connects us to the universal soul. Pranayama calms down the nervous system. Also, Pranayama energises the nervous system. Pranayama offers a multitude of physical, emotional, and the mental health benefits. Practising Yoga leads to the union of individual consciousness with the universal consciousness. Yoga creates harmony, i.e. the balance between the mind and the body, and the man and the nature. Pranayama is the Yoga of regulation of breath. Pranayama has certain breathing patterns, techniques and exercises. Pranayama is an exercise for physical and mental well-being. Eight types of Pranayama exist according to the Hatha Yoga, which make the body and the mind healthy. These eight types are Surya Bhedana (right nostril breathing), Ujjayi (victorious breathing or ocean breathing or psychic breathing), Sitkari (cooling breathing), Shitali (cooling breathing), Bhastrika (bellows breathing), Bhramari (humming bee breathing), Murch'cha (swooning or fainting breath) and Plavini (gulping breath). Three stages of the breathing in Pranayama are inhalation or Puraka, pause after inhalation or holding or retention or Antara Kumbhaka, and the exhalation or Rechaka. Pause after exhalation or suspension after air is being exhaled and before next inhalation begins, is known as Sunyaka. Five types of Prana, which are responsible for all pranic activities within the body are Prana (the Respiratory System), Apana (the Excretory System), Vyana (the Circulatory System), Udana (the Nervous System) and the Samana (the Digestive System). Prana and Apana are most important Prana. Prana is upward flowing breath or energy and Apana is downward flowing breath or energy. Prana is the energy, which moves up and inward. Prana is the energy, which leads us to our source. Higher the Prana, more cloistered one becomes in his or her inner world. Apana is outgoing breath. Apana is descending energy in the astral spine. Astral spine is the non-physical spine. Astral spine is more energetic as compared to the physical spine. The astral spine is the primary channel of the life-force within the body. Flow of the Prana (the rising energy in astral spine) and the Apana (the descending energy in astral spine) prompts lungs to breathe. Pranayama is a precursor or a preparatory practice, required prior to more advanced techniques of Pratyahara, Dharana and the Dhyana, leading to the ultimate stage of Samadhi. Pratyahara is withdrawal of senses. Dharana is concentration. Dhyana is meditation. Samadhi is enlightenment. Kapalabhati Pranayama is first Pranayama. Kapalabhati Pranayama is a skull shining breathing technique. Kapalabhati Pranayama warms up the body. Dirga Pranayama is a three part breath technique, which builds deeper awareness of body, breath, and the mind through their connections. Five Pranayama, viz. Anulom-Vilom Pranayama (Nadi Shdodhana or alternate nostril breathing), Bhramari Pranayama, Ujjayi Pranayama, Kapalbhathi Pranayama and the Bhastrika Pranayama should be a part of one's daily fitness programme. Bhastrika translates as Bellows. Bellows are the instrument, which produce a strong gust of air for fanning the fire. Bhastrika Pranayama cures hypertension, asthma, heart disease, TB, tumors, BP, Liver Sirrhosis, Sinus, and other energy and lungs related ailments and problems. Practice of the Pranayama modulates various activities of brain regions like Amygdala, Anterior Cingulate, Anterior Insula and Prefrontal Cortex. Amygdala is involved in emotions processing. Early morning is the best time to practise Yoga. Pranayama is best practised in morning on an empty stomach. Practise Pranayama for at least 15 minute at the same place and time, every day. In Pranayama Yoga, repeat 3 to 5 cycles before returning to regular breathing, and then, continue to alternate between nostrils. While in Pranayama Yoga, allow the mind to focus on the breathing patterns, and on the sound of the breath. The secret of Pranayama lies in dealing with female and male energies of central nervous system. During alternate nostril breathing (Anulom-Vilom Pranayama or Nadi Shodhanam), we alternately breathe through left and right nostrils, and thus, activating right and left hemisphere of the brain. Anulom-Vilom Pranayama involves holding one nostril closed, while inhaling, and then, holding the other nostril closed, while exhaling it. Take steady breath in through both the nostrils. Inhale until lung reaches its capacity. Maintain a tall spine during the Pranayama. Pranayama increases the defensive ability of the lungs.

CHAPTER TWENTY-ONE

Sudarshan Kriya

Sudarshan Kriya is a Sanskrit language phrase. Sudarshan Kriya means "proper vision by purifying action". Sudarshan Kriya Yoga (SKY) is a breathing-based meditation technique. Sudarshan Kriya is an advanced form of rhythmic and cyclical breathing, with slow, medium, and fast cycles. Sudarshan Kriya cleanses the body from inside. In Sudarshan Kriya, practitioner practises three different paces of breathing one after the other. Practitioner starts with slow-paced breathing, and then, does medium-paced breathing, and ultimately, finishes with the rapid-paced breathing. Since, Sudarshan Kriya comprises breathing at different paces, therefore, diaphragm gets strengthened. SKY strengthens respiratory muscles, which in turn, increases the excursions of diaphragm, and also, the lungs, along with increased thoracic compliance. The deep inhalations and exhalations regulate breathing and improve lung capacity. Sudarshan Kriya increases the flow of oxygen to the brain, and thus helps in focussing better. After Sudarshan Kriya, exultation is being experienced by the practitioner. Rhythm of the body and the mind is brought into sync by the Sudarshan Kriya. Final steps of Sudarshan Kriya are mediation and the relaxation. Creativity finds its expression through the Sudarshan Kriya. Meditation channelizes the energy by harmonizing the senses. Meditation is "becoming alive again". Meditation takes the practitioner back to the serenity, which is his or her true nature. Relaxation is very important yogic practice, which makes the practitioner calm and free of all worries. Sudarshan Kriya reduces stress and anxiety. Sudarshan Kriya positively affects the brain activities. Sudarshan Kriya leads to a better, memory, attention and emotional control. Sudarshan Kriya helps the practitioner to achieve a higher cognitive state. Sudarshan Kriya makes the brain quiet, by reducing impacts of overstimulation of the frontal lobes. Sudarshan Kriya increases Respiratory Sinus Arrhythmia (RSA). RSA is heart rate variability in synchrony with respiration, as a result, R-R interval of ECG gets shortened during inspiration, and prolonged during expiration. RSA relieves mental health issue like depression. Also, RSA regulates the levels of stress hormones in the body of its practitioner. Sudarshan Kriya increases alertness. Sudarshan Kriya must be taken as a part of morning routine. Sudarshan Kriya must be done on an empty stomach. To practise the Sudarshan Kriya, first do Ujjayi, or the victorious breathing, as it is a slow breathing, with 2 to 4 breaths per minute. Ujjayi allows, consciously experiencing the breath touching the throat. Sudarshan Kriya raises the prana, and also, the energy levels of its practitioner. Breath has much greater secrets of the life, the universe, and the God. Breath is the life. Breath is everything. Quality of breath and breath-process affects the life. After the Sudarshan Kriya, thoughts become fully positive. For a happy and meaningful life per se, it is very important to give attention to the spiritual aspects of the life, i.e. the Spirituality; the sacred cow of Yoga, and "Mediation inside the Pyramid". By the practise of Yoga, and Meditation inside the Pyramid, and the Spirituality, a chicken-hearted being becomes brave, decisive and resolute. Efforts and the courage, when in the right direction and for a right purpose, yield right intended results. Time is a created thing. Nature does not hurry, and yet, all things are well-accomplished.

CHAPTER TWENTY-TWO

Yoga Nidra

Yoga Nidra means the Yogic Sleep, or the Psychic Sleep, or the Effortless Relaxation. Yoga Nidra is one of the easiest Yoga Asana. Asana is a certain way of sitting or standing, while practising Yoga. Yoga Nidra is a conscious sleep, means sleeping yet conscious. Yog Nidra is a state of consciousness between the wakeful state and the sleep state, or the dream state (a state of half-consciousness), wherein, deep constructs of mind become opened. Yoga Nidra is far superior to the ordinary sleep. Yoga Nidra is "going-to-sleep", induced into a being through the guided meditation. Guided meditation is the meditation, led by a teacher, in person either through means of audio or the video. During the Yoga Nidra, one is made to enter into a calming state of the mind and the body, and thus, promoting self-awareness. Yoga Nidra is a rejuvenating sleep. Yoga Nidra creates physical and mental activities, which change the brain waves in order to release the emotional tension. Yoga Nidra slows down the nervous system. Yoga Nidra allows the muscles to relax. Yoga Nidra positively affects all five layers or the Koshas or the Sheaths, viz. the Physical Layer or the Annamaya Kosha or the Physical Sheath (related to food), the Energy Layer or the Pranamaya Kosha or the Life Force Sheath (related to energy), the Mental or the Emotional Layer or the Manomaya Kosha or the Mental Sheath (related to mind), the Higher Intelligence Layer or the Vijnanamaya Kosha or the Wisdom Sheath (related to intuition), and the Bliss Layer or the Anandamaya Kosha or the Bliss Body (related to the essence of one's true self or the nature, which is perfection). Yoga Nidra is suitable for anyone. A 30 minutes Yoga Nidra practicse is equal to 2 to 4 hours of good sleep. Yoga Nidra is practised from a position of total relaxation, known as the Corpse Pose, which is laying flat on the back. Yoga Nidra reduces the stress and gives deeper rest and relxation to its practitioner. Yoga Nidra induces restful sleep. Yog Nidra relaxes the muscles for a mindful-sleep. Every day practise of Yoga Nidra builds a healthy sleeping pattern, and cures insomnia, chronic pain, depression and anxiety. In Yoga Nidra, one does not lose his or her consciousness, yet the entire body, the mind and the nervous system get complete rest through deeper relaxation. Yoga Nidra manages immune function, blood pressure and Cortisol levels. Cortisol or Hydrocortisone (Cortisol made in the laboratory) is a hormone, which is made naturally by the Adrenal Cortex, the outer layer of the Adrenal Gland. Cortisol helps the body to use glucose (sugar), proteins, and fats. Hydrocortisone is used to treat inflammation, allergies, and cancers. Yoga Nidra practise removes excess Cortisol, which is a stress hormone, and which weakens the Hippocampus and makes a being vulnerable to depression and anxiety. Hippocampus is the elongated ridge(s) on the floor of each lateral ventricle of brain, which is the centre of emotion, memory, and also of autonomic nervous system. During Yoga Nidra practise, both Gamma-AminoButyric Acid (GABA) and Serotonin are naturally released in the body, and thus, creating both anti-anxiety and anti-depressant effects. GABA is an amino acid, which serves as primary inhibitory neurotransmitter in the brain. GABA is a major inhibitory neurotransmitter in spinal cord. Serotonin is a compound present in blood platelets and serum. Serotonin constricts the blood vessels, and thus acts as a neurotransmitter. Neurotransmitter is a chemical substance, which is released at the end of a nerve fibre by the arrival of a nerve impulse. Neurotransmitter is diffused across the synapse or junction, and thus, affecting transfer of impulse to another nerve fibre or a muscle fibre, or to some other structure. Yoga Nidra can be practised in the morning after Asana or Meditation, or before going to the bed. Yoga Nidra can be practised at any time, except, right after the eating. Eight stages in practising Yoga Nidra in a row are Settling or the Initial Relaxation, Intention, Body Rotation, Breathing and the Energy Awareness, Sense-Perception, Visualization, Sankalpa, and the Externalization. While practising the Yoga Nidra, position the head to make it rest comfortably. Then, close the eyes. Relax the eyelids by letting them simply lie on eyeballs, and do not squeeze eyelids to shut. Take a couple of deep breaths, while emphasizing the exhalation. Start everyday of the life with positive Sankalpa, and thus, use the Power of Intention for, self-growth, and the soul evolution. Yoga Nidra improves mindfulness. Through Yoga Nidra, which is a state of deep conscious relaxation, one heals him or her, restores, and awakens to his or her true potential. Yoga Nidra raises being's consciousness, and helps a being in getting enlightenment.

CHAPTER TWENTY-THREE

Bhakti Yoga

Bhakti Yoga is also known as, "the Bhakti Marga". Bhakti means "devotion" or "love" or "to adore or worship the God". Bhakti is deep yearning to experience the love, the love in its purest and the highest form, and then, to unite with that, which is eternal and unchanging. Bhakti Yoga is a Spiritual Path, or a Spiritual Practice. Bhakti Yoga is union with the supreme through love and devotion. Bhakti Yoga is a path to self-realization. Bhakti Yoga is experiencing oneness with everything. Bhakti Yoga is focused on loving devotion towards personal deity. The ultimate goal in the practice of Bhakti Yoga is to reach the state of Rasa (essence), which is a feeling of pure bliss, achieved in the devotional surrender to the Divine. Three classical paths, leading to Moksha, are Jnana Yoga, Karma Yoga and the Bhakti Yoga. Moksha is release from the cycle of rebirth. Moksha is a transcendent state, which is attained as a result of being released from the cycle of rebirth. Cycle of rebirth is impelled by the Law of Karma. Bhakti Yoga is the Yoga of love and devotion. Bhakti Yoga is a practise of selfless devotion and recognition of sacred or divine in everything. Bhakti Yoga is the path of self-transcending love or complete devotion to the God. Along with chanting and external offerings, have the courage to face self at the deepest levels. Offer everything to the Divine, both, the good, and the bad; do not hold anything back, as it is only the complete dedication and surrender. Only it is the true worship. Bhakti Yoga expands one's devotional awareness, and transforms his or her life, which then gets filled with peace, love, joy and harmony. We love others for the divinity that resides within them. God is pure consciousness. Bhakti Yoga is both, the means and the end, and allows us to use all of our senses, all our emotions, and all our actions to express love for everything. Treat others, the way we would like to be treated. Imbue all actions with an attitude of love, reverence and the devotion. Divine love is selfless and giving. Heal and nurture the relationships. Accept own faults. Forgive others. There is always grace in love, called as forgiveness. Bhakti Yoga transforms the life, from mundane to sacred, from trivial to profound. Bhakti Yoga prepares our hearts and minds to start receiving grace of unconditional love and wisdom. In Bhakti Yoga, being becomes an instrument of the Divine, and then, everything which he or she does, is an expression of love and devotion, and the life becomes a joyful celebration. Bhakti Yoga is practised by chanting songs of praise to the Divine, or setting up an altar with a favorite image or representation of the Divine and offering flowers, fruits, or incense, or simply doing mental worship. Meditate on chosen image of the God. Visualize the image of the God in heart or in the space between the two eyebrows. Concentrate on it. Create a relationship with the divine, say of a loyal friend, or of a loving parent, or of a devoted lover. Pray every day, especially the prayer of gratitude. Be thankful for all aspects of the life, whether difficult, or the pleasant. Appreciate the wonder and beauty of the nature. See the nature as a manifestation of the Divine. Purify thoughts and actions by practising Yamas and Niyamas. Yamas, and their complement Niyamas, represent a series of ethical rules, meaning "reining in" or "control". Yamas and Niyamas are restraints for proper conduct, and they are a form of moral imperatives and commandments. Practice forgiveness and the compassion. Accept self-fault, and also, the fault(s) of others. Help others. Be humble. Offer food to the Divine before eating or sharing a meal. Keep observing patterns of mind, emotions, and practices. Channel emotions through positive creative means. Bhakti Yoga is simply falling in love. Bhakti Yoga is love. Bhakti Yoga is the path of devotion towards all humans and animals.

CHAPTER TWENTY-FOUR

Jnana Yoga

Jnana Yoga, or the Gyana Yoga, is also known as Jnana Marga, or the Gyana Marga. "Jnana' means knowledge or wisdom. Jnana Yoga is one of the three Yogas or Trimārga or three soteriological paths or three classical paths for Moksha or salvation for liberation of human spirit, viz. Karma Yoga or the Karma Mārga (the path of action), Bhakti Yoga or the Bhakti Mārga (the path of devotion to Ishwar or God), and the Jnana Yoga or Jñāna Mārga (the Path of knowledge). Jnana Yoga emphasizes the "path of knowledge", also known as the "path of self-realization". Yoga is a spiritual practice, which emphasises introspection, leading to the self-development. Jnana Yoga is the path of awareness through absolute consciousness by practising Svadhyaya (self-study). Jñāna Yoga pursues knowledge with questions like "who am I, what am I, what is myself (soul)", along with the many other intriguing and mystical questions of the life and the existence. Jnana Yoga takes a being on a journey toward full self-knowledge and the enlightenment. Four pillars of Jnana Yoga are Viveka, Vairagya, Shatsampat and the Mumukshutva. Viveka refers to the discernment. Vairagya refers to the detachment and dispassion. Shatsampat refers to six virtues of mental practice to balance mind and invoke discipline. These six virtues of Jnana Marga are Sama, Dama, Uparati, Titiksha, Shraddha and Samadhana. These qualities are brought into the personality by practising the Yoga, which manage the mind to see the self. Sama refers to tranquility of the mind. Sama or calmness means not reacting to any external stimuli or action. Dama means controlling the senses. Dama or strength doesn't let mind fall prey to any sensory stimuli. Uparati refers to satiety. Uparati means fulfilling all worldly duties wholeheartedly. Titiksha means endurance. Titiksha is enduring all pain and suffering in silence. Shraddha means faith. And, Samadhana refers to balance with attention. Samadhana is a single-minded focus on supreme liberation. Mumukshutva refers to longing or yearning. Three types of Jnana are Mati Jñāna, Śruta Jñāna and the Avadhi Jñāna. Mati Jñāna is sensory knowledge. Śruta Jñāna is scriptural knowledge. And, Avadhi Jñāna means clairvoyance. Three phases of Jnana Yoga are Sravana, Manana and Nididhyasana. Sravana refers to exposure to knowledge, like reading a book or listening to a lecture or simply watching a video. Manana means revisiting the knowledge for further understanding. And, the last phase Nididhyasana is the phase of experimentation. Jnana Mudra or Gyan Mudra or Dhyana Mudra is a gesture of intuitive knowledge. Veils of illusion are created by notions, concepts, world views, and the perceptions. Jnana Yoga utilizes one-pointed meditation on a single question of self-inquiry to remove such veils. Thus, Jnana Yoga practice allows one to realize the temporary and illusionary nature of Maya. Maya is the power by which the universe becomes manifested. Maya is illusion or appearance of the phenomenal world. A being practising Jnana Yoga sees the oneness of all things. The knowledge gained by practising Jnana Yoga helps one to realise his or her selfish desires, limitations, ego, illusions, and the ignorance. Jnana Yoga liberates a being from sufferings, by attaining the experiential knowledge of absolute divine truth and the universal consciousness. Jnana Yoga makes one to get rid of everything, which is superficial, and the being becomes a self-realised being. Self-realisation is fulfillment of one's own potential. To practise Jnana Yoga, sit in a comfortable position, and assume a pose or a posture say Padmasana. Lotus position or the Padmasana is simply a cross-legged sitting meditation pose, in which each foot is placed on the opposite thigh. Other poses like Ardha-Padmasana or Sukhasana or Vajrasana can also be assumed. Spine must be kept straight. In Ardha-Padmasana or the Half-Lotus pose, only one foot is put at the top of the opposite, while keeping the other foot under the out-stretched thigh. Ardha-Padmasana is an easier version of Padmasana. Sukhasana, is a very easy pose, which is performed in a seated position. Sukhasana pose is entered by first sitting on the floor, and then, folding the left leg, until it is touching the right thigh. Then, the right leg is folded, such that it touches the left thigh. Hands are kept on the knees. The spine should remain erect, and breathing must be normal. Do not assume Sukhasana pose in case of any severe leg problem. Also, do not practise Sukhasana pose, if there is any pain in the lower spine, or in Sciatica, or with knee problems. Vajrasana or the Thunderbolt Pose or the Diamond Pose, is a kneeling Asana. Asana is the way of sitting or standing, while practising Yoga. In Vajrasana, kneel and then sit back on legs so as to take the weight off the knees. After assume a suitable pose, open up palms, and touch the tips of thumb and the index finger. Keep rest of the fingers straight of both the hands. Rest the palm on knees, while keeping the face looking upwards. Now, calm the mind. Make the mind free of all emotions, feelings, and the worldly thoughts. To calm the mind, take a few deep breaths. Even if mind strays, do not get harsh on it; instead, guide it gently towards the mindfulness. Once the mind is devoid of thoughts, follow the six steps viz. Sama, Dama, Uparati, Titiksha, Shraddha and Samadhana, which help in stabilizing all emotions, and also help in differentiating the true self or the real self from all that which is transient, fleeting and impermanent. While practising Jnana Yoga, one can even ask him or herself existential questions about the inner self. After following these six steps, meditate for as long as feeling comfortable. End the session of practising Jnana Yoga by the process of Palming, i.e. rubbing the palms together quite vigorously. Once the palms get sufficiently warm, place them on the closed eyes for a few seconds, and then, remove palms, and gently open the eyes. Jnana Yoga practise stills the mind and keeps all unwanted thoughts away. Janana Yoga is an excellent technique of mindfulness for reducing stress and anxiety. Reduced stress lowers risk of hypertension, headaches, heart diseases, high blood sugar levels etc.. Jnana Yoga channels the flow of energy within the body, and also leads to the conscious breathing. Jnana Yoga improves the blood circulation, and when, circulation improves, organs like kidneys, liver, heart etc., function much better than before. Thus, Jnana Yoga also prevents serious diseases related to kidneys, liver, heart etc.. Jnana Yoga Mudra (Jnana Yoga pose), involving touching the tips of thumb and index finger together, also works as a technique of Acupressure. Acupressure is a form of Alternative Medicine, i.e. a therapy, in which manual pressure is used for stimulating specific points on the body, along what are considered to be the lines of energy. Acupressure makes the pituitary and the pineal glands healthy. Acupressure reduces risks of hormonal imbalance and thyroid. Alternative Medicine is a range of medical therapies like Herbalism, Naturopathy, Crystal Healing etc.. Janana Yogra practise improves focus and creativity. Jnana Yoga induces self-realization. Jnana Yoga helps realising full true potential, which also helps achieving all personal and professional objectives. Jnana Yoga frees its practitioner from any baggage and all illusions, which is quite essential to let true personality and inner-self shine through. Jnana Yoga is the Yoga of kindness and the compassion, which focuses on the serving the self. All outer experiences are essentially created inside. Work on the inner in order to make the outer world better and beautiful. Living a meaningful life is an art, which very few know, and practise towards it. Practise the Yoga, do Meditation inside the Pyramid, and be the blessed one, and eventually become a very powerful soul. Be a couth true seeker of the truth, and not just a lout rubberneck.

Karma Yoga

Karma Yoga is the path of action, which can be either mental, or physical, or both. Actions create memory(s). Karma is memory. Karma is both action, and also, the result of action. Three types of Karma are Prarabdha, Sanchita, and Kriyamana or the Agami. Prarabdha Karma is experienced through present body. Prarabdha Karma is only a part of Sanchita Karma. Sanchita Karma is the sum of one's all past Karma. Kriyamana Karma or the Agami Karma is the result of current decisions, and the actions. Karma Yoga is one of the most practical and effective means of spiritual development. Karma Yoga is about performing actions, and offering services from the heart, with full attention and awareness, and without any fruitive desires. Karma Yoga is the path of action without attachment(s). Attachment to the outcome(s) of actions, when something is expected in return, brings suffering. When there is no expectation, there is peace. Karma Yoga frees us from the bondage of sufferings. Karma Yoga practitioner must act with no expectations. He or she should serve others positively and selflessly without thinking of the results. Karma Yoga is an act of mental discipline. Karma Yoga is a discipline of selfless action, as a way to the perfection. Beings, which act in the ways as prescribed by the Karma Yoga, transcend the cycle of karma, and the momentum of cause and effect, which perpetuate life situation of perceived identity. Karma Yoga involves full acceptance of the Dharma, i.e. one's duties in the life with no selfish motives and desires. Karma Yoga is also known as the Karma Marga. Karma Marga is one the four spiritual paths, which is based on the "yoga of action". The others three spiritual paths are Jnana Yoga, Rāja Yoga and the Bhakti Yoga. For a Karma Yogi, i.e. the practitioner of Karma Yoga, right selfless action is a form of prayer and a connection with the divine. Karma Yoga annihilates the ego of its practitioner. Karma Yoga dissolves the sense of separation between the self, and the others. Karma Yoga purifies the mind. Karma Yoga is, having certain attitude towards the action, and is not any action. Motive towards the action(s) must be always righteous. Mantra chanting can also be done while engaging in the Karma Yoga. One's Doshas must be balanced. Dosha is a Sanskrit language word, which means fault or defect or simply that which darkens. In Ayurveda, Dosha indicates the excess, which causes disease(s). In Ayurvedic medicine, Dosha refers to each of three energies, viz. Vata, Pitta, and the Kapha, which circulate through the body, and govern its various physiological activities. Differing proportions of Doshas determine being's temperament and physical constitution. Unbalanced Doshas cause a disposition to certain physical and mental disorders within the being(s). Impurities of mind are called the Mala. Mala motivates to act in the interest of self-gain. Selfish attitude makes us forget that we are much more than our bodies and emotions, and the identity, which minds think of us to be. We are consciousness, which illumines our bodies and minds. As

Mala loosens, a connection to deeper truth in the heart is re-established. Karma Yoga is about performing the duty without thinking about the self. Karma Yoga controls, and eventually, let us go off our ego. Ego leads to the attachments, and the desires, in the life. Four principles of Karma Yoga are, the right attitude, the right motive, giving up the result(s), and the serving. Karma Yoga purifies the mind, and cleanses the heart. Karma Yoga promotes positive feelings like humility, kindness, benevolence, compassion, charity, honor, esteem, gratefulness, generosity, love, and the joy. Kindness is the ultimate karma. Karma Yoga eliminates negative emotions like envy, hatred, fear, greed, selfishness, and jealousy. Karma arises due to the desires. A Karma Yogi never neglects his or her duties and the responsibilities. Actions govern the existence. Renunciation does not mean an escape from duties and responsibilities. Engage minds in contemplation. Beauty catches attention, whereas, character catches hearts. Life is a journey between the two states, of "human being", and of "being human"; therefore ensure your thoughts and actions bring you closer to the latter with each passing day. Never fash for anything in the life, have faith and belief in the God, and the self.

CHAPTER TWENTY-SIX

Kriya Yoga

Kriya Yoga means "Yoga of Action". Yoga and Meditation require self-discipline. Kriya Yoga is about the spiritual growth. Kriya Yoga lengthens the span of its practitioner's life. Kriya Yoga is a meditation technique, which speeds up the spiritual process of its practitioner. Kriya Yoga creates awareness and promotes the self-consciousness. Kriya Yoga accelerates practitioner's pace to meet his / her higher self. Kriya Yoga controls energy through Pranayama and Meditation. In Kriya Yoga, breath is being paused. We all are born with a certain number of breaths. And if, breath can be paused, life duration of a being gets extended. Breath is the Prana, i.e. the life force. Stretching (Ayama) every breath (Prana) is the Pranayama. One cycle of breath includes one inhalation (Purak), and one exhalation (Rechak). "Stretching" means, putting a pause (Kumbhak), after the inhalation, and before the exhalation. In normal adults, 12 to 15 breath cycles occur in a minute. Breath or the Prana is the age or the duration of the journey of life. Kriya Yoga is quite technical, and involves many steps. In Kriya Yoga, heart activity is also paused. Kriya Yoga improves the bone-health. Leaving the mind, is the state of suspended animation. Bringing stillness to the body is the first step in practising the Kriya Yoga. Kriya Yoga conserves the energy. Kriya Yoga makes the body to take the minimal inputs and maximise its outputs. Anti-ageing (reverse the ageing, or the anti-oxidation) processes get kicked-in by the practise of Kriya Yoga. There are four ways or techniques to do the Kriya Yoga, viz. through spiritual action(s), by using discriminatory wisdom, through self-effacing love, and through Meditation. Thus, Kriya Yoga is an effective blend of four paths, viz. the Karma Yoga, the Jnana Yoga, the Rāja Yoga, and the Bhakti Yoga. Five branches of Kriya Yoga are, the Kriya Hatha Yoga, the Kriya Kundalini Pranayama, the Kriya Dhyana Yoga, the Kriya Mantra Yoga, and the Kriya Bhakti Yoga. Kriya Yoga is done in seven steps, Step 1 basic practise of Meditation, Step 2 mind focussing, Step 3 heart opening or the devotion, Step 4 receiving guidance and grace from / of a Guru, Step 5 expanding the awareness, Step 6 preparation, and Step 7 the initiation. AUM Technique can be used for the expansion of the awareness. Neti Kriya is an example of the Kriya Yoga. There are four types of Neti Kriya, viz. Sutra Neti (using a string), Jala Neti (using the water), Dugdha Neti (using the milk), and the Ghrita Neti (using clarified butter known as Ghee). Sutra Neti is practised with a string. Jala Neti, Dugdha Neti and the Ghrita Neti are done with a Neti pot to deliver the liquid into the nostril. Sudarshan Kriya Yoga is the Kriya Yoga breathing. Kriya Yoga breathing involves Ujjayi, Bhastrika and AUM chanting. Ujjayi or the Victorious Breath involves experiencing the conscious sensation of the breath, while touching the throat. During Bhastrika or the Bellows Breath, air is rapidly inhaled and forcefully exhaled at certain rate usually 30 breaths per minute. AUM is chanted three times with prolonged expiration or the exhalation of the breath. Kriya Yoga is the path of self-realisation. Kriya Yogi understands the mechanics of life-making. Yoga and Meditation are just magical in all their effects.

CHAPTER TWENTY-SEVEN

Hatha Yoga

Hatha Yoga is a power Yoga for self-transformation. The Sanskrit word Haṭha means "force". Hatha Yoga means the "Discipline of Force". Hatha Yoga is also known as Shatanga Yoga. Shatanga Yoga means six-limb-yoga. Hatha Yoga is a system of physical exercises and breathing control. Hatha Yoga uses physical techniques to conserve, preserve and channel the vital force or the energy. Hatha Yoga stresses the mastery of the body. Hatha Yoga aims at attaining a state of spiritual perfection in which mind is withdrawn from the external objects. A Hatha Yogi experiences the union of all polarities. Hatha Yoga Asana practice is categorized into three components, viz. standing, sitting, and finishing. Hatha Yoga, through a disciplined practice of, Asana (postures, Mayurasana, i.e. Peacock Pose), Pranayama (breath control, Anuloma Viloma), Mudra (manipulations of vital energy, Viparita Karani), Bandha (energy locks, shutting off the flow of energy to specific parts of the body) and the Shatkarma (purifications, Nauli), unites mind, body, and the spirit. Body-centric practices strengthen and purify the physical body, and also, cultivate the Prana, i.e. the life-force energy. Hatha Yoga activates Kundalini, the dormant spiritual energy. Hatha Yoga is made up of three main practices, viz. body postures, breathing techniques, and the meditation. In Hatha Yoga, body is moved slowly and deliberately into different poses, which challenges the strength and the flexibility. And, at the same time, there is full focussing on relaxation and the mindfulness. Eight limbs of Yoga are Yama, Niyama, Asana, Pranayama, Pratyahar, Dharana, Dhyana and the Samadhi. Yama means the abstinence. Niyama is the observance. Asana refers to the Yoga postures. Pranayama means the breath control. Pratyahara is the withdrawal of senses. Dharana means the concentration. Dhyana is the meditation. Samadhi refers to the absorption. Yoga teaches discipline. Discipline means following the path of religion in the life. Real religion of being is, "being and becoming". In God's "No" for an answer, there is always a greater "Yes", behind it. God's "No" is never a rejection, but always a redirection. Love the beings, and not the things. Beings are made to be loved. Things are made to be used. Do not use the beings. In the absence of loved ones, there is no meaning of any success and wealth and position in the life. Also, failure has not much impact on the being, if there are loved ones around him or her. Value the beings. Value the relations, and the relationships. Relations and the relationships are the gifts of the life. Fears of a being, force him or her, to live a very miserable life. Everything, which is aspired for, by the being, is on the other side of his or her fear. Mountains of fears are not meant to be carried, but meant for climbing and crossing on to its other side. Life is a painting, created with the lines of hope, mistakes being erased with tolerance, and the brush dipped with patience to bring along the colours of love. In the life, everything gets okay, when we get okay with everything. Be compassionate and kind. Kindness is more than the deeds.

Kindness simply lifts the other being(s). Kindness is an attitude, an expression, a look and a touch. In the life, all those things, which challenge us, also change us. Hatha Yoga makes the sleep better. Hatha Yoga strengthens the core muscles. Hatha Yoga cures the depression, and eliminates the stress. Hatha Yoga improves the balance and the core strength. Hatha Yoga relieve neck and back pains. Hatha Yoga strengthens the flexibility. Hatha Yoga enhances mindfulness. Hatha Yoga is about consciously holding on to an Asana, which alters the way of thinking, feeling and experiencing. Hatha Yoga is a sport, a science, which uses the body and the postures.Terrible times wreak havoc on the ongoing life of beings, but it is always their tests, the tests of their life, conducted by the God. Life is designed like that. And, the purpose is, to teach new lessons, add new experiences, and to make the being stronger. No event is good here, and no event is bad here. All is just a drama; the drama of the life, the drama of the existence. Nothing is for real here, and all is too ephemeral. Explore the real side of yours, the life's and the nature's. Enjoy the pageantries of the life. Do not hold on to the bad past, and the bad, times, experiences and the memories. Cherish good memories. Only the good, is germane to the progress and growth, peace, joy and the happiness, in the life, and it will helps to remain ebullient and exuberant. Stay filled with joie de vivre. God's grace is the only refuge or only place to get ensconced.

CHAPTER TWENTY-EIGHT

Sahaja Yoga

Sahaja Yoga teaches self-realization or Moksha (enlightenment) through awakening of the Kundalini energy, i.e. a dormant energy within the body. Word "Sahaja" means spontaneous. Sahaja Yoga restores the inner balance, and brings a sense of well-being. Sahaja Yoga improves self-esteem. Sahaja Yoga revitalizes the energy within. Sahaja Yoga restores optimism in the being. Sahaja Yoga brings peace and the contentment in the life to its practitioner. Sahaja Yoga develops the ability to self-regulate the attention, and thus, focussing on the present. Sahaja Yoga fosters curiosity, openness and acceptance. Kundalini is the divine power within all of us. Kundalini is a form of divine feminine energy. Kundalini is located at the base of the spine in the Root Chakra (Muladhara). Kundalini energy rests like a coiled serpent at the Muladhara. When Kundalini energy flows freely upward through the seven chakras, i.e. seven energy centres, then it leads to an expanded state of the consciousness, which is known as Kundalini Awakening. For awakening the Kundalini, first dress up for comfort, and then, begin by tuning-in for getting into a meditative frame of the mind. Focus on the third eye chakra. Use a mantra. Focus on the breath. Add Mudras (postures). Divide breathing into equal segments. Again and again, return attention to the breath, if it wanders. While practising the Sahaja Yoga, its practitioner feels divine vibrations in his or her hands. Sahaja Yoga connects the inner-self with an eternal spirit, which is the source of peace and joy, and the true knowledge. In addition to the physical body, beings have a subtle body too. Subtle body is made up of energy channels (Nadi) and the energy centres (Chakra). Absolute truth can be felt and understood through this energy system. Sahaja Yoga improves the awareness effortlessly, and thus, creating mental, emotional and the physical balance. Sahaja Yoga meditation works directly on the Central Nervous System. Central Nervous System controls all mental, physical and emotional activities. Raising the Kundalini takes the practitioner into a state of thoughtless awareness. It simply takes the practitioner beyond the mind. Raising the Kundalini allows its practitioner to evolve into a state of much greater awareness. The practitioner feels, a gentle release from his or her mind, and a spontaneous state of the bliss. The practitioner merely witnesses and enjoys the present moment. It is the state of utter mental silence. Kundalini rise removes strains occurring on the Central Nervous System. These strains cause negative mental, emotional, or physical sensations. Rise of Kaundalini brings the whole system into a balance and sync. With the regular practice of the Sahaja Yoga Meditation, the Central Nervous System is regularly cleansed, and thus, it becomes more resistant to the imbalances. Practitioner is evolved into, a centred, a highly satisfied, and a very loving being, and he or she gets close and closer to the essence of his or her true self. Be in the state of peace and silence. Silence is very powerful, as silence is of the cosmos. Silence establishes being's spirit's connection with the universe and its various powers. We are neither the body nor the mind, but we are the spirits.

CHAPTER TWENTY-NINE

Raja Yoga

Raja Yoga is a form of Yoga, which intends to achieve control over the mind and the emotions. Raja Yoga studies the human mind. The practitioner of the Raja Yoga becomes aware of his or her mind's habitual tendencies. Raja Yoga is the path of, self-discipline and practise. In Raja Yoga, the practitioner controls the mind, desires, breath, and the body. Raja Yoga eliminates being's ego. Raja Yoga has eight, limbs or the stages, viz. the Yamas, the Niyamas, the Asana, the Pranayama, the Pratyahara, the Dharana, the Dhyana and the Samadhi, leading to the self-realization, and the liberation. These eight limbs or stages are called the Ashtanga. Yamas means the restrictions. Niyamas refers to the observances. Asana means the pose. Pranayama is the breath control, i.e. control of the vital energy. Pratyahara means the withdrawal of senses. Pratyahara is drawing mind's focus away from all external senses towards the inner sensations of the body. Dharana means the concentration of mind. Dhayana means the meditation. And, the Samadhi is attainment of the super-conscious state. Raja Yoga focuses on the Meditation and the Energetics. Energetics is the branch of the science, which deals with the properties of the energy, the way in which energy is redistributed in the physical, the chemical, and the biological processes. Raj Yoga frees the mind from negative chatter and self-limiting thoughts. Raja Yoga eliminates stress, anxiety, and panic. Raja Yoga builds the self-confidence. Raj Yoga elevates the state of mind. Raja Yoga makes its practitioner feel positive. Raja Yoga improves the quality of life. To do the Raja Yoga Meditation, firstly be in a comfortable seated position, and then, obtain a slow deep breath. After that, begin practising the internal limbs, viz. the Pratyahara, the Dharana, the Dhyana, and the Samadhi. Raja Yoga is the practise of identification of the mind with the infinite, and the expansion of the consciousness in all directions.

CHAPTER THIRTY

Beej Mantra Meditation

Beej is a Hindi word, meaning "the seed". Beej Mantra is also known as the Seed Mantra. Beej Mantra is a monosyllabic Mantra. Daily meditation with Beej Mantra(s) balances the energy of Chakra(s). Beej Mantra calms and focuses the mind. Beej Mantra stabilises the flow of the Prana. Beej Mantra harmonises the five elements, the Pancha Bhuta. A Beej Mantra is an abridged Mantra. It is the reason why it is called a Beej. A Mantra or Mantram, is a word, or just a prayer, which is chanted or sung. Mantra is a syllable, a sacred utterance, a numinous sound, phonemes, a word, or a group of words. A Beej Mantra is a short one syllable word, which is chanted to cultivate concentration, mindfulness, and the state of meditation. Beej Mantra contains the essence or seed energies of specific deities, the elements of the universe, and the entire cosmos. Beej Mantra are very powerful and too energetic in their nature. Beej Mantra can be chanted individually. Beej Mantra can also be found to be contained in the longer Mantras. Mantra contains magical religious and spiritual powers. "Aieem" or "Aim" is a Beej Mantra, having one syllable, associated with the goddess Saraswati. The Goddess Saraswati is a Hindu

Goddess of knowledge. Goddess Saraswati represents the principle of divine wisdom in the nature. "Aum" is the basic Beej Mantra. Aum is further expanded into several types of Beej, viz. the Yog Beej, the Tejo Beej, the Shanti Beej, and the Raksha Beej, also known as, the Aieem or the Aeng or the Aim, the Hreem, the Sreem, the Kreem, the Kleem, the Dum, the Gam, the Glaum, the Iam, the Yam, the Aam or the Um or the Ram. Each Beej Mantra has ability to resonate with the vibrations of a specified Chakra, having the resonance frequency of 110 Hz., or 220 Hz., or 440 Hz., or 880 Hz., or 1760 Hz., or 3520 Hz.. Beeja Mantra chanting connects its practitioner with the universe, and its energies, i.e. the cosmic energy. Chanting these sacred seed sounds affects the mind. Beej Mantra chanting affects subtle energy centres of the subtle body. Beej Mantra chanting strengthens the spiritual power. Beej Mantra chanting improves the awareness of being in the present moment. Thus, Beej Mantra activates channel specific frequencies of sound vibrations in the body and the mind. Beej Mantra, when recited, gives the being(s), a lot of positive energy. Beej Mantra creates a certain vibration. Beej Mantra represents the call of the soul. Beej Mantra contains the essence of the deity. Beek Mantra invokes the deity. Beej Mantra directly addresses the deity. Beej Mantra is sound manifestation of the deity. Chant Beej Mantra regularly in the prescribed way to enhance the spiritual power. Chant the Beej Mantra while sitting or walking. By chanting the Beej Mantra, the devotee gets wisdom, knowledge, fortune, happiness, courage, strength, protection, success, elimination of all fears, and protection from enemies, and above all, the divine protection. There is a certain Beej for every deity. Three types of Beej Mantra are the Shakti Beej Mantra, the Element Beej Mantra, and the Chakra Beej Mantra. Shakti means power, strength, endurance, and energy. Chanting a Shakti Beej Mantra awakens the Kundalini, the life force energy, which lies dormant at the base of the spine. One can tap into the cosmic elements and the divine feminine energy Kundalini by chanting the Shakti Beej Mantra. Shakti Beej Mantra is associated with the Kali, the Durga, the Parvati, the Lakshmi, and the Saraswati, the primary forms of the goddesses. Therefore, Shakti Beej Mantra is very helpful for women, wishing to activate their inner strength, courage and the confidence. Shakti Beej Mantra contains the power of transformation, which affects the deepest layers of the consciousness, the Kundalini and the Prana. Shakti Beej Mantra should be chanted with utter respect, full concentration, immense devotion, and great caution. Shakti Beej Mantra, "Aum" or "Om" is associated with the Trinity, viz. the Brahma, the Vishnu and the Shiva. Shakti Beej Mantra, "Krim" or "Kreem" is associated with the Kali. Shakti Beej Mantra, "Shrim" or "Shreem" is associated with the Lakshmi. Shakti Beej Mantra, "Hrim" or "Hreem" is associated with the Durga. Shakti Beej Mantra, "Hum" or "Hoom" is associated with the Shiva. Shakti Beej Mantra, "Aim" or "Ayeim" is ssociated with the Saraswati. Shakti Beej Mantra, "Strim" or "Streem" is associated with the Tara. And, the Shakti Beej Mantera, "Klim" or "Kleem" is associated with the Krishna. The five elements or the Pancha Bhuta of a Beej Mantra evolve from five the Tanamatras, i.e. the principles, viz. Earth from Gandha (smell), Water from Rasa (taste), Fire from Rupa (sight), Air from Sparsha (touch), and the Akasha from Shabda (hearing). Beej Mantra activates the Chakra inside the body. There is a specific Chakra Beej Mantra for every chakra. Tanmatra is a Sanskrit word. Tanmātra are rudimentary, undifferentiated, subtle elements of the existence from which gross elements of existence are produced. A Mantra can be incorporated into any form of meditation. Transcendental Meditation and the Metta Meditation also make use of Mantra. Vedic Mantras are some of the oldest forms of chanting. Beej Mantra "Aum" or "Om" is mentioned in the Indian scriptures, the Vedas, the Upanishads, and the Mundaka Upanishad. From the basic and foundational sounds of the Beej Mantra, more elaborate and more complex Gayatri Mantra has emerged. To activate the power of one of the five elements or the Pancha Bhuta, viz. fire, water, earth, air, and the space or the ether, choose a specific Element Beej Mantra. Chanting Element Beej Mantra purifies negative emotions. Also, the Element Beej Mantra cleanses the aura, and promotes healing. These elemental sounds of Element Beej Mantra are manifestations of primordial forces of nature, embodying the qualities of element. Element Beej Mantra for earth promotes energies, which are solid, stable, grounded, and stable. Element Beej Mantra for water invokes a liquid, fluid, flowing, and the changeable energy. Beej Mantra of the five lower chakras corresponds to each one of the five elements. Each of body's seven chakra or the energy centres has a one-syllable Beej Mantra, which activates its vitality and the latent power. Intoning a Chakra Beej Mantra accelerates or decelerates the flow of energy associated with that charka, and thus causing the chakra to intensify and get purified. While chanting a Chakra Beej Mantra, focus the awareness on the position of the chakra along the spine. Chakra Beej Mantra chanting moves and harmonises the flow of energy inside, and makes the practitioner to feel connected, radiant and joyful. Chakra Beej Mantra, "Lam" is associated with the Muladhara Chakra and the element earth. Chakra Beej Mantra, "Vam" is associated with the Svadhishthana Chakra and the element water. Chakra Beej Mantra, "Ram" is associated with the Manipura Chakra and the element fire. Chakra Beej Mantra, "Yam" is associated with the Anahata Chakra and the element air. Chakra Beej Mantra, "Ham" is associated with the Vishuddha Chakra and the element space or the ether. Chakra Beej Mantra, "Aum" or "Om" is Associated with the Ajna Chakra. Chakra Beej Mantra, "Ha" is associated with the Sahasrara Chakra. The sacred vibrations of Beej Mantra, strengthens the connection with the divine, which helps in tapping the higher states of consciousness, where the wisdom resides. Beej Mantra Meditation provides a sense of clarity, inspiration and motivation, calmness, focus, peace, love and joy, and protection. Regular Beej Mantra chanting reduces stress, lowers the blood pressure, and increases the energy levels. Beej Mantra syllables have healing powers. Group chanting of the Beej Mantra creates a collective resonance, which amplifies the power of words (Beej or the seed). Beej Mantra chanting activates channel specific frequencies through sound vibrations, which stabilises the flow of Prana, harmonises the five elements and makes the mind calm and focussed. These sound vibrations stimulate specific points, and the energy centers on the body, to open up and release the blocked energies, and thus bringing all seven Chakras into the state of balance. We beings (the Vyashti) are elements of the society (the Samashti). Society is an element of the nature (the Srishti). And, nature is an element of the God (the Parameshti). Forgiveness is the characteristic of a strong being, as a weak being can never forgive. There is a need for clear and deeper understanding of the life, ubuntu (humanity to others), no misbehavior, and no the exploitation. Every morning seen in the journey of the life is a new beginning, a new and a renewed hope, a blessing. Life is better in the company of good beings. Add life to the each day of the journey of life, and not the days to the life. Never do cheap gossips and backbiting. Do prayer(s) regularly. Do not get jealous. And, do not show off and swagger. When we get hurt, do not take it other way; rather take it this way that the life is trying to teach something. Always, resistance to the change is painful. Change is never painful. Learn and grow every time. Life, nature and the existence are the teachers. Keep moving in the journey of life. Life is a big drama. Nothing is real here. Nothing remains here. Everything in the creation is changing and evolving continuously, so is, its design. Never look back, and see what has been done, but see, what remains to be done. Control the mind. Win over the mind. Mind causes all evils. Mind is the biggest friend, and also, the biggest foe. Leave footprints of kindness and love with each step taken in the journey of life. Manage the life, learn life management. Become silent, when in anger. Be honest, and act honestly, when in trouble. Be simple, if rich and wealthy. Be polite, when in authority. These are tests of worthiness of a being by the God. Life is a test. A being, which is simple, is peaceful. To remain happy in the life, have a childish heart, no matter how old are you. Always, keep smiling. Panpsychism (the doctrine or the belief that everything has an element of individual consciousness) holds in this creation. Treat every other thing here in this vast existence with great respect; it costs nothing, but earns us everything. Completely surrender to the God, with full faith and belief in the God, and then, miracles will start happening in the life. In the state of complete surrender to the God, i.e. the self-dissolution, laws of nature do not work. Law of Gravitation does not work in this state. Law of Electricity and Magnetism also does not work in the state of complete surrender (zero ego state). The Beej Mantra should be chanted with focus, concentration and devotion. The Beej Mantra Meditation fulfils the desires of its practitioner, and acts like his or her protective shield, surrounding him or her all the time, and protecting him or her from various dangers and enemies. Meditation unifies the whole nervous system. The Beej Mantra Meditation promotes a happy and a healthy life. We are not, what happens to us, but, we are, what we choose to become. Do not slam, but be panegyric. The secret of good health is to live in the present moment and enjoy it. Feel the pains of others, as only those, who are alive, can feel the pain, and a dead, can never feel the pain.

CHAPTER THIRTY-ONE

Angel Meditation

Angels like Afriel, Ariel, Cassiel, Charmeine, Dina, Gabriel, Gavreel, Michael, Raphel Uriel etc., are the divine positive beings, which keep surrounding all of us all the time. Angels listen to us, and take interest in almost everything in our life. Angel Afriel is the angel of youth. Angel Ariel is the angel of nature. Angel Cassiel is the angel of temperance. Angel Charmeine is the angel of harmony. Angel Dina is the angel of learning. Angel Gabriel is angelic messenger. Angel Gavreel is the angel of peace. Angel Michael is the angel of loyalty. Angel Raphel is the angel of the spirits of men, and it heals the earth. Angel Uriel is the angel of wisdom. Archangel is the chief angel of greater than the ordinary rank. Raphael, Michael, Gabriel and Uriel are archangels. Archangels Raphael, Michael, Gabriel, and Uriel represent air, fire, water, and the earth, respectively. Miracles happen in the life. Angels create these miracles in our lives. Angels love us, care us and protect us. Angel meditation connects the beings with the angels. Meditation becomes easy and more effective inside the Pyramid. Meditation is the process of establishing communication with the universe. Angel meditation is the meditation for inviting the angels, interacting with them, taking suggestions, messages and guidance from them. Sit comfortably and straight, for the

Angel Mediation. Keep body well hydrated. Connect with the breaths. Experience the peace. Inhale the happiness, and exhale all worries of life. Imagine an expanding engulfing light. This light corroborates the presence of angels. Connect with this light, as it is the connection of the self with the angel(s). Entreat message(s) from the angel. Plead the angel for a solution of a problem, or some kind of help, and it will come immediately from the angel, in this state of the Angel Meditation. No being's life is perfect, as there are always some or other problems. Life is all about the right towards. No problem is the end of the world, but always a new and a different beginning, of a more beautiful and exciting life, with much enhanced understanding, and the increased strength. In the show and the game of the life, have the needed expertise, prowess and the gravitas. Be the author of a panegyric on the Life and the God.

CHAPTER THIRTY-TWO

Anapana Sati Meditation

Anapana Sati Meditation is a breathing meditation. It leads to the enlightenment. Anapana is the first step of the practice of Vipassana Meditation. "Anapana" means observation of respiration, as it comes in, and goes out. "Sati" means mindfulness. Anapana Sati means mindfulness of breathing. Mindfulness is the mental state of being conscious or simply aware of something. Mindfulness is achieved by focusing the awareness on the present moment. Mindfulness is a therapeutic technique. Anapana Sati Meditation increases the level of Serotonin. Serotonin is a chemical compound, which is present in the blood platelets and the serum. Serotonin acts as a neurotransmitter. Serotonin carries messages between nerve cells in the brain, and also, throughout the body. Serotonin affects the mood, digestion, nausea, wound-healing and blood-clotting, bone-health, and the sleep. Sleep is a natural unconsciously performed meditation. Sleep heals the mind, the body, and the spirit. Anapana Sati is the meditation for stillness of body and the mind. Anapana Sati Meditation focuses on in-and-out breathing. There are sixteen stages in Anapana Sati Meditation.

Anapana Sati Meditation improves mood, health, psychology, relationships and the performance. It is a relaxing meditation. Anapana Sati Meditation improves inter-hemispherical communication between the two hemispheres of the brain. The practitioner of this Meditation becomes happier and positive by doing this meditation. It brings the peace of mind. It improves self-actualisation. Self-actualisation is the realisation or the fulfillment of one's talents and potentialities. Anapana Sati Meditation brings job satisfaction. Ananpa Sati Meditation improves being's immune system, airflow to the lungs, blood pressure, headaches, and migraines. Anapana Sati Meditation lowers the risk of cardiovascular diseases in the beings. Anapana Sati Meditation prevents depression, anxiety, and stress. Anapana Sati Meditation controls being's emotions. Anapana Sati Meditation improves energy flow within the body of the being, which is practising it. Anapana Sati Meditation further increases sympathy, compassion and love. Anapana Sati Meditation improves the memory. It increases the focussing power and the cognitive abilities, and thus, leads to increase in the productivity. Anapana Sati Meditation has been propounded by the Buddha, and it works on, and improves, the mindfulness (Sati), concentration (Samadhi), tranquility (Passaddhi), energy (Viriya), equanimity (Upekkha), rapture (Pity), and the investigation (Dhamma Vicaya). One should always choose a good place, neither hot nor cold, which is also secluded, quiet and peaceful, and comfortably lit, for practising the Anapana Sati Meditation. The place for practicing Anapana Sati Meditation must be free from all distractions. Pyramid is the best place for it. Practise this Meditation inside the Pyramid. Sit up straight and comfortably, such that head and neck are in line with the spine. Relax. Now, concentrate the mind only on breathing. Connect to the mind, and to the breath. Concentrate on the sensation caused by the breath between the lips and the nose. Feel the energy of the breath. Breath is the life force. Inner stillness will be experienced along with the power and the freedom. Count every breath cycle, i.e. breathe-in and breathe-out for some time. Breath alters the state of mind. Now, advance further, once the focus on breathing has been maintained. Observe the thoughts, and identify the self, i.e. the true self or the real self. What other beings think about you is not important, but, what you think about yourself means everything to you; remember it. Aum chanting can also be done in the Anapana Sati Meditation. Feel the connection and the sync among the mind, the body and the spirit. Do Anapana Sati Meditation each and every day, for that much minutes, as much is your age. Anapana Sati Meditation is meant for the best upkeep of the physical body, the mental body, the emotional body and the spiritual body. Disease is absence of energy in the cells of the body. Anapana Sati Meditation sends the energy to such weak cells in the body. Aura gets strong by doing Anapana Sati Meditation. Anapana Sati Meditation changes the quality of life, and takes us on a journey from commonalty to the divinity. Anapana Sati Meditation conserves and preserves the inner energies by completely stopping its otherwise unnecessary dissipation.

CHAPTER THIRTY-THREE

Vipassana Meditation

Vipassana means the "insight." Vipassana Meditation is a form of mindfulness meditation. Vipassana Meditation is a way of self-transformation, achieved through the process of conscious self-observation. The "Power of Concentration" furthers through the practise of the Vipassana Meditation. Vipassana Meditation is a way to get free of all bondage, and liberate. Vipassana Meditation is a way of observing oneself without any judgement. Anapana Sati Meditation is the first step in the practise of the Vipassana Meditation. Anapana Sati is important to attain an abiding calm or the Samatha. Samatha practice is fixing the mind on a single object without moving. Vipassana Meditation develops the insights, which follow the attainment of the Samatha. One can't skip the one, and only do the other; however, depending upon the practitioner's level, he or she can choose to focus on one, more than the other. Vipassana Meditation focuses on a deeper interconnection between the mind and the body. In the Vipassana Meditation, the practitioner pays attention to the physical sensations. Physical sensations validate the existence of the body. Also, physical sensations interconnect the body and the mind, and condition the mind. Vipassana Meditation helps in achieving the enlightenment. It is a mental balancing practice. In Vipassana Meditation, one should totally abstain from, killing any being, stealing, sexual activities, telling a fib, and intoxication. Vipassana Meditation rests on the concepts of Anicca i.e. the impermanent nature, Dukkha i.e. the suffering, and the Anatta i.e. the selflessness. Annica, Dukkha and the Anatta are natural phenomena. Without any realisation, Annica, Dukkha and the Anatta are going on within every being, every moment. Vipassana Meditation practitioner seeks to understand the things as they truly are. Vipassana Meditation practitioner observes the world in a state of tranquility, awareness, and the mindfulness. Vipassana Meditation aims at removing all distractions using the consciousness. Distractions prevent a being from seeing the reality. Through Vipassana Meditation, its practitioner achieves liberation or a state of the enlightenment. For doing Vipassana Meditation, set aside 10 – 15 minutes every day. Select a comfy and quiet place with very few distractions. Sit comfortably, preferable on the ground. Breathe normally. Watch each breath. Reach a state of zero thought first, and then, become mindful of physical sensations. Also, be mindful of the thought(s) that are trying to enter the mind. Allow all these thoughts to pass without judging or analysing these. Continue with this practice. Focus on the inner consciousness. Keep maintaining attention on the breath for the rest of the meditation. In Vipassana Meditation, practitioner needs to sit around all day long, and learn to sharpen the awareness; awareness at the level of sensations. Vipassana Meditation practice has two major activities sets, viz. the Observation, and the Control. Four stages of Viapssana Meditation are, the Sotāpanna i.e. the stream-enterer, the Sakadāgāmi i.e. once-returner, the Anāgāmi i.e.

the non-returner, and the Arahant. Vipassana Meditation offers multifold health benefits, and eliminates, blood pressure related problems, mental problems, and depression and anxiety. In the life, everything big and good is hard before it is tried, and then, it becomes very easy. Hardships in the life, prepare the being for a good destiny and an extraordinary life. Life is a bioscope, where all its events and the stories are totally untrue. Goal of the life is not necessarily becoming the best, but necessarily trying the best. Life is about, the love, relations and the relationships, and the God. Become good, and rizz up all and everything in this existence. Do not lead an illusory life, but always live in the awakened state. Vipassna Meditation practise is a journey from agitation and miseries towards the peace and the happiness. Peace comes from within. The only thing, which a being should do in his or her life, is to work on, "the self", in order to know it and improve it, and then, to use it for every good and greater purpose. Never elicit scant sympathy out of solipsism and lack of self-awareness.

CHAPTER THIRTY-FOUR

Aum Chanting Meditation

Aum or Om symbolises the conscious or the waking state. Aum also symbolises the universe, i.e. the ultimate reality. Aum is the most basic Mantra. Aum is a very sacred syllable, which contains three sounds in it, viz. the sound 'a', the 'sound u', and the sound 'm', which refer to the continuity of the past, the present, and the future. Aum is the sound of the creation. Aim is an unlimited eternal sound. Aum is a sacred sound; the sound of the universe. Aum encompasses all other sounds within it. Chanting Aum, is calling the God, Aum chanting also affirms that we are the God. 21 Aum should be chanted; five for the organs of actions (hands, feet, vocal chords, elimination organ anus, and the generative organ), five for the organs of perception (eyes, ears, nose, tongue, and the skin), five for the five vital airs of the body (the Prana in lungs, the Apana the flatus moving downwards through rectum, the Vyana diffused throughout the whole body, the Samana at the navel essential for digestion, and the Udana rising through throat up to the head), five for the five encasings or the sheaths of the body (the sheath of intellect, the sheath of vital air, the material sheath, the mental-emotional sheath, and the sheath of bliss), and the last one Aum for the practitioner itself for his or her self-realisation, i.e. fulfillment of own potential. Elongate the word Aum by focussing on the first sound, and then, keep gape opening the mouth as you move on to the last part of the Aum. Keep lips together, while chanting the Aum. Then stay silent for some time, till it is time to repeat the chant again. Spend around 80 percent of breath chanting sounds "A-U," and around 20 percent of breath chanting sound of the syllable, "M." Continue this Aum chanting meditation till you find that you are in sync with your breath. Aum chanting can be done for about 20 minutes. Aum chanting can be done in three ways, viz. through, mouth, mind and one's wholebeing. Wholebeing refers to recognition of that, which we each live. Each one of us lives within three worlds, i.e. the inner world of mind, the world of physical body, and the world outside (the nature). The sound of Aum, when uttered, originates in the belly, and vibrates in the upper chest, of the practitioner. Aum chanting improves concentration. Aum chanting improves the memory. Also, Aum chanting restores the balance of mind and the energy of the practitioner. Aum chanting is quite calming and relaxing. Aum chanting eliminates all stress. Aum chanting raises the vibrations by increasing the frequency and the energies. Aum chanting is refreshing. Aum chanting maintains a healthy rhythmic heartbeat. Aum chanting cures heart and blood pressure related diseases. Aum chanting clears and opens up sinuses. Aum chanting balances out the hormonal secretions like Endorphin, which cause mood swings. Sometimes, it is OK, to not to be OK. Humans are sentient beings. Humans are cogs in a wheel; the wheel of the existence, i.e. the whole creation. Emotional intelligence is the key to the success in the life. Live for a better and much greater cause and the purpose, than the ordinary and the mundane. Give up all bad, habits, thoughts and actions, cold turkey. Also, do not let the problems seem larger than life. Smooth seas do not make skilled sailors. The more you are burnt, the more you get purified, and become a better you. What we seek, also seeks us. Believe in the Power of Belief and the Power of Meditation. Meditation has the power of healing. Meditation does magic, and creates miracles in the life. Dinero does not bring happiness. Meditation simply makes the being, ecstatic. Dhayana or the Meditation becomes several times easy and powerful inside Pyramid. Cosmic energy is focussed on being doing meditation by the Pyramid inside it. One can easily see his or her past life during meditative state inside the Pyramid. Failures are the part of life. One, who has never failed, simply means that he or she has not tried anything new, exciting and the adventurous. Success and the failure, are merely the two experiences of the life, rather one experience only, as one lies into another. Faith works for simple people with plain minds, and not for too much thinking people. Meditation inside a Pyramid is classic instance of science meeting the nature. We are the creators.

CHAPTER THIRTY-FIVE

Raja Yoga Meditation

Raja Yoga is the path of discipline, which focuses the mind of the practitioner. Raja Yoga is also known as the Ashtanga Yoga due to its 08 limbs. The Raja Yoga Meditation is a form of meditation sans rituals or the mantras. Raja Yoga Meditation is practised with open eyes. Raja Yoga Meditation can be practised anytime and anywhere. The Raj Yoga Meditation enables the practitioner to reach the illustrious king (Raja) within, i.e. the supreme self. Raja Yoga Meditation is a royal path leading to the divinity. The practitioner of the Raja Yoga Meditation experiences serenity and the bliss. Raja Yoga Meditation is a communion of "I" with the true self, i.e. the God within, leading to utter contentment. Raja Yoga Meditation improves the relations and the relationships, eliminates stress and anxiety, and improves the sleep quality. Raja Yoga Meditation improves memory and the powers of attention and concentration. Raja Yoga Meditation eliminates jitter, and chatters of the mind, and thus, makes the mind, quite clear and focussed. Raja Yoga Meditation trains the mind to become self-actualised and self-realised. Self-actualisation is the highest level of being's psychological development, where being's true potential is fully realised after fulfilment of his or her basic bodily and ego needs. Raja Yoga Meditation develops a sense of well-being within its practitioner. One can very easily overcome all his or her bad and the negative habits with regular practise of the Raja Yoga Meditation. To practise the Raja Yoga Meditation, focus on the breath, lift the chest while inhaling, and allowing the belly to expand. And, while exhaling, press the navel towards the spine, and press the air out of lungs very slowly and steadily. Eight limbs of Raja Yoga Meditation are, the Yamas, the Niyamas, the Asanas, the Prānāyāma, the Pratyahara, the Dharana, the Dhyana, and the Samadhi. Yamas means restraints like Ahimsa, i.e. the non-violence and the non-injury. Niyamas refers to the observances, observing the requirements of rules, morality, rituals including the Saucha, i.e. internal and the external purity. Asanas is a body posture, a steady pose, a balancing pose or any position like sitting, standing, reclining, inverted, and the twisting. Prānāyāma is the yogic practice. Prānāyāma practice focuses on the breath. In Sanskrit, the word Prāṇa means the "vital life force". In Sanskrit, the word Yāma means to gain control. Thus, Prānāyāma is a technique of gaining control of the vital life forces. Breath is associated with the Prāṇa. Pranayama elevates the Prāṇa Shakti, i.e. the life energies. Pratyahara refers to the withdrawal of senses from the external objects. Dharana means the concentration. Dhyana means the meditation. And, Samadhi is the state of superconsciousness. Superconscious is the aspect of mind, which accompanies the conscious, the subconscious, and the unconscious. Superconsciousness is a blissful state. In the state of superconsciousness or the Samadhi, practitioner perceives him or herself, and the full existence, with a pure, holistic, and intuitive awareness. Raja Yoga is the Yoga of the mind and the body control. Raja Yoga focuses on the Meditation and the Energetics. Energetics is the branch of science. Energetics deals with the properties of the energy, and also the ways of the energy, in which the energy is <u>redistributed</u> in various physical, chemical, or the biological processes. Raja Yoga is also a planetary and a celestial state, affecting the mind, the body and the spirit. Raja Yoga is formed, when the trine planets are exalted and posited in their own houses. Trine is an aspect of 120°, i.e. the one third of a circle. Venus trines the Mars. Jupiter trines the Pluto. When planet Jupiter conjuncts with the planet Moon in Lagna, and also, the Sun is placed in Kundli, the phenomenon gives rise to the state of Raja Yoga. Such a being develops religious nature, and earns lots of power, fame, money and wealth in his or her life, like a Raja (king). Lagna or Lagnam is related to an individual time and the place of birth. Lagna or Lagnam differentiates between two beings, which are born on the same day and same time, but at the different places, i.e. different longitudinal divisions, or two beings born on same day and same place, but at different times of the day. Kundli is the Birth Chart or the Horoscope. Kundli is an astrological diagram. Kundli evaluates one's future, and gives out predictions about him or her. To create one's Kundli, his or her birth's date, time and place, data or the information are needed. By regular practise of the Raja Yoga Meditation, the practitioner gains 08 powers, symbolised by the eight petals of the Lotus. Thus, Raja Yoga Meditation is the practice of the systematic analyses of the mind, and gaining the control over the mind. Hatha Yoga, Kundalini Yoga, and the Mantra Yoga are parts of the Raja Yoga. One's negative attitude emanates bad energies, which is his always off-putting. The Raja Yoga Meditation offsets all negatives, and develops a right and the positive attitude, and the gravitas, in the being. The Raja Yoga Meditation is a far-out Meditation technique.

CHAPTER THIRTY-SIX

Golden Ball Meditation

The Golden Ball Meditation is a Yoga based Meditation technique. In the Golden Ball Meditation, the practitioner visualises or imagines a golden light ball at the centre of self. Golden light signifies the brightness, which comes from the sun; the fire. As we inhale, this golden light ball expands in all directions. Then take a pause, and feel this golden light ball within. As we exhale, send light of this golden ball throughout the body. Golden Ball Meditation eliminates stress and anxiety. Golden Ball Meditation improves the mental and the physical healths. Golden Ball Meditation improves the immunity. Golden Ball Meditation improves the quality of sleep. Golden Ball Meditation improves focus, concentration and the self awareness, and brings new hopes filled with the joy and the happiness. Meditation rejuvenates all body cells. Health of the cells of the body is the health of the being. Four pillars of Meditation are awareness, connection, perspective and the potential. Approach, practice and integration are the three aspects of the Meditation. Earth, Water, Fire, and the Wind representing the qualities of solidity, cohesion, temperature, and the motion, are the four elements of Meditation. Grief is the price, which we pay for the love. Maintain probity all through the journey of life, as it is the sine qua non for peace, joy, happiness, good overall health, and the enlightenment. Practise mindfulness for a better future. Meditation unfolds the mysteries of the life. Meditation is the magic, making the miracles to occur in the life. Meditation makes the soul happy. Love yourself.

CHAPTER THIRTY-SEVEN

White Light Experience

Three types of lights in this universe are absolute, virtual and the polarity. Each of these lights produces specific and powerful effects on the life. White Light is a mix of all wavelengths of visible spectrum, whether occurring naturally, or artificially. White Light is the space, 5th, 6th, and 7th dimensions, in this existence, which houses positive energies. Illusion of time exists up to 4th dimension. Whatever enters into the White Light realm or the space, comes out perfectly clean and pure. White Light is called on for the purpose of healing, uplifting the vibrations, protection, and the assistance. White Light balances the Chakras. White Light is the light of the divinity. White Light denotes purity and the quality. White Light is neither harmful, nor can be harmed. White Light is available to all. White Light is easily accessible, provided one is open to receive it. White Light Experience cleans the Aura. After cleaning the Aura, impurities, which have been combed out of the Auric Field should be sent towards the White Light for cleansing. Saints, Angels, Ascended Masters, Permanent Living Masters (PLMs), our Higher-self and the Lightworkers, are the agents of this White Light. Negative and dirty energies are sent towards the White Light for the purpose of purification and the transformation. Astral

Plane, the plane of dreams and nightmares, and the Akashic Records, is 4th dimension of the consciousness or the spiritual realm. 7th dimension is a pure state of being. White Light Experience is a meditation-based stimulation of pineal gland. Pineal gland is situated deep into the brain. It is the "third eye". Visions of White Light indicate that the third eye is getting opened. The White Light Meditation and Experience is visualisation of a radiant white light, which enters the head from the top, and then, moves down through all seven Chakras. Thus, the White Light Experience cleanses and heals the entire being. Stop living in the routine. Mundane is monotonous. Stop doing the same mundane thing every single day. Spend time with others. Pray to the God. Do the Meditation and the Yoga. Live the life, as the God intended. To practise the White Light Meditation and getting its experience, sit in a quiet place, in an upright position, with spine, back and neck straight. Soft music can also be played. Indulge in Meditation. Rest the hands on the thighs. Bring tips of both thumb or index fingers or middle finger in touch. Thumb signifies the willpower. Index finger signifies the leadership. Middle finger signifies the individuality. Ring finger signifies the affection. And, the pinky finger signifies the bonding. Meditation develops five strengths or power in the practitioner, viz. energy, faith, mindfulness, concentration and the wisdom. Always, choose your words very carefully. Do not hurt anybody and anything in this creation. Earth, a 3-dimension physical plane, is a melding pot for karmic balancing. Here, in this creation, every other thing, every other being, is me only, i.e. just another you or me. Life is a celebration, celebrate it - carpe diem. Do Yoga and the Meditation, improve Aura, create positive vibrations, send positive energy, exhibit positivity, and attract everything to you, the like moths to the flame. Being's pitiful squeals must tug at heartstrings; be compassionate. Beings have jejune opinions about the life; be exuberant. No being is a minnow, but a priceless creation of the nature. Gyan (knowledge), Bhakti (devotion) and Karma (action) are the three essentials of a meaningful life.

CHAPTER THIRTY-EIGHT

Transcendental Meditation

Transcendental Meditation (TM) is a Meditation technique for detaching oneself from anxiety. TM practise increases the levels of Serotonin in beings, whose Serotonin is low, thus depression is alleviated and eliminated. TM promotes harmony, and leads to the self-realisation. TM is a silent Mantra Meditation. TM improves, the focus, the awareness, the memory, clarity of the mind, quality of sleep, intelligence, creativity, productivity, and the self-esteem. TM is a mind technique, which works at the subtler levels of the mind and the intellect. TM is the Meditation technique, which takes the practitioner beyond the mind and the intellect. For practising the TM, sit very comfortably on the floor, or in a chair. Keep both the hands on the lap. Close the eyes for a few seconds up to a minute or even more. Take few deep breaths. Relax the body. And, silently repeat a Mantra in the mind. Do it for 15 - 20 minutes. Mantra aids to the concentration in the Meditation. Mantra is words or phrases or visualizations, used during a meditation to help calm the mind. Do it until you reach a state of the inner peace. In TM, there are exclusive Mantras, which help achieve a state of perfect stillness and consciousness. TM technique is quite simple and effortless. There are immense physical health, mental health, cognitive and emotional benefits of TM.

CHAPTER THIRTY-NINE

Chitta Shakti Meditation

Chitta is the pure intelligence. Chitta is the mind without memory. Chitta Shakti is the primordial cosmic energy, which governs all mental functions. Everything, which happens in the life, is as per the Chitta. Chitta is simply there, everywhere, in the cosmos. 16 dimensions of human mind fall into 4 categories, viz. Buddhi (the intellect; the brain), Manas (the memory; the data and information), Ahankara (the sense of identity), and the Chitta (the cosmic intelligence). Buddhi is the logical dimension of thought. Buddhi is the first dimension. Buddhi, to work, needs the Manas. Manas is the second dimension. Manas has many layers. Manas is spread all-over the body, and thus, creating a sheath, known as the Manomaya Kosha. Every cell in the body has memory, known as the Cell Memory. Cell also, has the intelligence, but no intellect. Intelligence is built by gaining information and gathering the knowledge gradually, through external means like books, teachers etc.. Whereas, the intellect is developed through individual efforts. Intellect is developed by exercising the faculties of questioning, thinking and the reasoning. Intellect does not approve anything sans logic basis or the reasoning. Ahankara is the third dimension. Ahankara is more than the ego. In the case of normal beings, which are not enlightened beings, Buddhi works within the sphere of the context, created by their Ahankara. Their intellect is seriously enslaved to their identity, whereas, the intellect of enlightened beings is not enslaved to their identity. It is desired that one should function much beyond and above his or her intellect. Chitta connects to the basis of creation within the being. Chitta simply connects the being to his or her consciousness, and is always ON, irrespective of the fact that one is awake or asleep. The intellect gets ON, when awake, and gets OFF, when asleep. The cosmos is a living mind, and the Chitta is the last point of the mind. Chitta makes the life to happen. Chitta is very powerful. Through the Chitta Shakti Meditation, the practitioner touches his or her Chitta, the fourth dimension of his or her mind, and then, the best possible things, which can happen to him or her, start happening anyway. Chit Shakti meditation is not just visualization. Touching Chitta, is also called as, "Ishwara Pranidhana", meaning, "God becoming slave"; thus working for you. Chitta Shakti Meditation is consciously accessing the Chitta. Chitta gives the permanent and true solution of a problem, where as the Buddhi may give temporary and false solution(s) to a problem. Buddhi confuses a being, but the Chitta, unclouds him or her. Chitta Shakti Meditation manoeuvres all energies in a specific direction. Power of Chitta is the Power of the Subconscious Mind. To do this Meditation, lie down on the mat, slowly lowering the spine down. Adjust to a comfortable position. The weight of body should be evenly distributed. Focus on the breath. Reach a state of Shoonya (zero). Shoonya Meditation is a process of conscious non-doing, thus, creating a distance between the real self and the body and the mind.

CHAPTER FORTY

Japa Meditation

Japa Meditation is also called the Mantra Meditation. Japa (जप) is a Sanskrit language word, which means, meditative repetition, of a Mantra, or of a divine name. Japa is done by uttering in a low voice. Japa Meditation involves chanting of a Mantra. Mantra or Mantram is word(s) or phonemes, a syllable, a sacred utterance, a numinous sound, which is repeated to aid the concentration in the Meditation. Mantra has religious, magical and the spiritual powers. Japa keeps the mind calm and steady, and also, resistant to the disturbance(s). Japa Meditation eliminates the stress. It creates specific brainwave states. Japa increases endogenous neural oscillations in Posterior Cingulate Cortex (PCC) in low frequency Delta-band. Combination of, deep breathing, sacred sound(s), and slow steady rhythm of Japa Meditation, becomes a very powerful spiritual dose. Beaded Mala is used in the Japa Meditation. During the Japa, chant a Mantra, and also, rotate or count or push-shift the beads of a Mala (a string of prayer beads). It will act as a point of reference for the awareness. After some time, the practitioner will naturally get into the rhythm, where movement of the beads of the Mala, gets synchronized with the chanting. Always keep Mala in a clean place, preferably in a Mala bag. Four types of Japa are the Vaikhari, the Upamshu, the Manasika, and the Lakhita. The Vaikhari Japa is done loudly or audibly. Upamshu Japa is whispering. Manasika Japa is mental, and the Lakhita is written Japa. Do Japa 108 times. There are 108 Marma points in the body. Marma points are the vital points of the life forces in the body. 108 times chanting of Mantra is a journey from the material self towards the highest spiritual self. Each Japa brings the practitioner closer to the God within, by 1 unit. Aum is good mantra to practice, in the Japa Meditation. The Mantra Japa creates positive mental tracks. Mantra Japa has transformative power and the energy. Mantra means "tool of thought", and the Japa means "muttering". Eschew bad thoughts and bad actions. Think good, and do the good, in the life. Every being needs downtime to unwind him or herself, and the best way is, to do the Japa Meditation, with full, trust, faith and the self-confidence. Confidence comes with the success, and the success comes with the confidence. Start believing in the self, then miracles will also start happening in the life. Have self-confidence, as it is the power; a superpower. Life is a miracle. Truth is the only authority. In the journey of life, some lines should never be crossed. Never focus on the problems, as otherwise, problems will start getting attracted in the life. Focus on the possibilities, as it has the ability to open more and more opportunities.

CHAPTER FORTY-ONE

Law Of Attraction

It is always a chicken - and - egg question, whether the matter or the energy, is the basis of the universe. And beings, often draw a blank about it. It's kinda abstruse and intrigue. Positive or negative thoughts bring positive or negative experiences into the life. Positive thoughts and positive actions attract and reap positive rewards in the life. Negative thoughts and negative actions attract and reap penalties in the life. Positive thoughts attract the positive events in the life. Negative thoughts attract the negative events in the life. The core of Law of Attraction is positivity. Law of Attraction is about thinking, creating, and allowing. The Law of Attraction is about attracting magnetic power of the universe. The magnetic powers of the universe manifest through every being, and also, through everything. Law of Attraction is about attracting the thoughts and ideas, people, situations and circumstances. The Law of Attraction manifests through the mind. Law of Attraction manifests through thoughts and imagination. Law of Attraction creates the reality in the life, which one wishes for. Law of Attraction works by visualizing mental image(s) of what we want to achieve, or simply by repeating positive affirmations. In this way, we create and manifest in our life, what we visualize or repeat in our mind. Repeating the same thought day after day, with full interest and intense feeling, makes the thought to materialize. Thoughts are very powerful. Like attracts like. Manifestation and Creation are in the core of the Law of Attraction. Through Manifestation, the practitioner can make the creative power of the Universe to manifest itself for creation of the things, which are needed in the life. Focus is the power. Have a very strong desire, and the faith, to manifest what we want in the life. Repeat the thoughts to be manifested in the life. Mind is the magnet. Change the bad thoughts with good thoughts, and the life will change eventually. Do not entertain negative thoughts, i.e. thinking about difficulties, problems, obstacles, hardships, worries, anxieties etc.. Quell negative thoughts and harbour the positive thoughts. We are the part of the universe's Law of Creation, as we have been created by the universe, and also, we have the ability, and the power to create further. Use this Power of Creation to bring the desired changes in the life, and make dreams come true. Law of Attraction brings the fulfilment of things, dreams, and the everything, in the life. Respect the life. Resist the evil. Never hurt others by your words, and also, through your acts or deeds. Control the thoughts. Control and manage the mind. Always work for good of all others. A being, who is happy, will keep others also happy. Being simple means being peaceful. Live with detachable attachments. Detachable attachment means that you own the things but nothing owns you. Do not think much, just act, do what is just, and also, you like, and above all, also makes you happy. In the book called, "The Wisdom", "Honesty" is its first Chapter. Always try knowing the truth. Be a seeker. Do not become a habitué to this earth. There are more pains than the pleasures, here in the physical realm. Habit of doubt is quite dreadful. Doubt is poison. Doubt ends the relations and the relationships. Learn, to forget, and to forgive. Let bygones be bygones. Try living with the God, i.e. the spiritual element and permanent, and not with the physical or the material, which is material and ephemeral, as there in the God's realm in the afterlife, we get everything. Life on Earth is a learning phase; a very short duration of the life. Do Meditation regularly, if possible, inside a Pyramid.

CHAPTER FORTY-TWO

Visualisation And Manifestation

Visualization is a great access point for the Meditation. Visualisation refers to the formation of the mental visual images. Position, color, size and shape are the basic elements of the Visualisation. Visualization is a certain process, which holds a mental image for the physical and the spiritual transformation. This mental image can be of, a symbol, or an event, or a place, or the God. Transformation means transformation of the mind; mind clarity, enlightenment, and a powerful connection to the sacred, or simply, unity with the God. Physical transformation relates to the healing. Visualisation process takes one deep and the deeper, within the self. Visualisation moves one deeper into the stillness and the spiritual depths. Visualisation establishes a connection with the higher power and the higher self. Visualisation increases the confidence. Visualisation brings the success. Visualisation eliminates anxiety and stress, and motivates the being to give his or her best performance. In Visualisation, one imagines every step of an event or an activity going very well, and thus, we make our mind and the body, ready to take those steps in our real life. The Third Eye Chakra is responsible for

Visualization. Visualisation re-programs the nervous system. For Visualisation, ask questions to establish what we are trying, and then, get the answer(s). Then, create a plan and choose the best type of Visualisation technique. Thus, Visualization Meditation is concentrating on a mental image in order to help focus and centre the mind and the body. Visualization activates creative powers of the subconscious mind. Visualisation makes the subconscious mind to work hard and harder at creating solutions to the problems of the life. Thus, Visualisation motivates the being and brings the success in his or her life. Manifestation is about bringing things into the reality. Law of Manifestation rests on the principle that through focus and supportive action(s), thoughts, beliefs, feelings and actions get transformed into the physical reality. Manifestation requires purposeful thought, actions, and the intention. Manifestation is about getting aligned to the feeling of what we wish to experience in the life. And then, through the energetic alignment of thoughts, feelings, actions and the emotions, these unreal virtual experiences are allowed to take the real form(s). Thus, Manifestation is the process of bringing or make happening something in the reality, through deliberate thoughts, actions, and the intention. Whereas, Visualization is practice of creating mental images or pictures of things wished for, in the mind. Visualization is about creating mental images in order to achieve a specific goal or an outcome. Visualization gives us clarity and focus. Visualisation allows us to take the necessary and desired steps to make dreams come true. Visualise the desired results. Visualisation develops positive beliefs and attitudes towards the success. Visualisation helps in comprehending how to manifest the life, as we wish for. Thus, one can very easily manifest things through the Visualisation. The 369 Method of Manifestation involves jotting down, what is to be manifested, three times in the morning, six times in the afternoon, and nine times in the evening. Visualise twice daily for about 10 minutes. Most effective Visualisation moments are waking moment, and the moment just before going to the sleep. Doing so engages the subconscious mind in our efforts towards the desired results and outcomes. Visualization is most powerful Manifestation technique. The "55 x 5 Method of Manifestation" is the Law of Attraction, which requires its practitioner to write the manifestation affirmations, 55 times per day, over the 5 days. Doing so, creates a realignment in the subconscious mind, and thus, making it to believe that biggest desires are already true and happening. 8 rules or the Principles of Manifestation, based on the Law of Attraction are, Visualisation, Believing, Feeling, Wanting, Receiving, Acting, and Enjoying. The "444 Rule of Manifestation" is also based on the Law of Attraction. Number "444" means that our practise of Visualisation and Manifestation is on the right path. The number "444" means that thoughts and actions are aligned with the highest good. Seeing the number "444" is a divine sign and symbol that Manifestation is happening, i.e. desires are getting converted into the reality. For Manifestation, be crystal clear in the vision with no fear and the doubt, correct the behaviour, express gratitude, turn envy into the inspiration, and have a strong unshakeable belief and trust in the universe. Realise the "Power of "Now"" in the daily life. Do it now. Do meditation now. Today makes the tomorrow. Present is the creation, and the outcome of the past. Present will create the future. Practise Xenoglossy. Xenoglossy or Xenoglossia or Xenolalia is a paranormal phenomenon, in which a being speaks, or writes, or understands a foreign language, which he or she has not acquired by the natural means. Xenoglossy is used for knowing the past life.

• 145 •

CHAPTER FORTY-THREE

Confidence

Confidence is the power. The Power of Confidence develops the ability within us to face any challenge of the life. Self-confidence is a great power. Confidence is developed by learning and the hard work, and by facing the challenges of the life. Dare to face the problem of the life, the problem will get convert into an experience, and then, into the solution, a piece of knowledge. Knowledge brings the confidence. No problem in the life is overwhelming, which a being just cannot handle. It is such a design of the life by the God. Different beings are subjected to different problems in their lives, depending upon their level of confidence and the ability to endure it. Ability brings the agility. Success depends on the confidence and the fortitude. Confidence is trust on self, and on the God. "Leap of Faith" brings good results of actions, only to those beings, which take it. Confidence comes from not fearing to be the wrong. Intent of actions only matters in the Game of the Life. Just be, what you are, and do not try changing yourself, as you are the best, the way you are born, and the things you are born with. Every being in itself is the unique and "the best" creation by the God. Say what you feel. Pent up emotions and feelings always vent, rather burst open at certain moment, in very unceremonious ways. Preparation is the key to the self-confidence. Kindness also creates and boosts the confidence. Confidence on self, is believing the self, which then, makes the magic and the miracles to start happening in the life. "I can", and "I shall", are the most powerful phrases for achieving everything in the life, which is wished for. Be optimistic. Use the Power of Subconscious Mind. Think positive. Pragmatism along with virtues and the morals is the only best way to lead a successful life. Do not limit yourself. Argue the limitations. Limitations are false creations of the mind. Challenge the mind. Life is all about the mind management. Confidence breeds the strength, which then, leads to the adventures. Do not try ever proving yourself to the other being, as it is endless, and also futile. You alone are enough. We come alone into this world, and also, go alone from this world. However, God is always with us. Confidence multiplies with every success, and the success needs the confidence. Confidence breeds the confidence through the successes. Confidence is always silent. Lack of confidence or the insecurities are always quite loud. Build self-esteem. Love yourself. Loving the self, is loving the God, and also, it builds the self-confidence. Trust that the universe loves you most, like any other being and the entity, no matter what, and this faith, is the key to the success and the happiness in the journey of life. Our connection with the nature is the connection with the universe and the God. Do Yoga and Meditation with full trust, faith, belief and the confidence, as it will solve all the problems of the life, be it physical or the mental, and expect the unexpected. Confidence gives the courage. Courage is, resistance to fear, mastery of fear, and not the absence of fear. Hope is the best support during the difficult times of the journey of life. It is the hope, which whispers in the ears, "all is well", and brings a smile on the face. Think good for others, in return, good things will naturally come to you in your life; it is the rule and the law of nature. Carry a happy-go-lucky attitude. Be happy with nothing, and you will then become happy with everything. Smile is the best make-up. Modesty is the best jewellery. Confidence is the best clothing. Positive mind is the best medicine. Health comes from, the peace of mind, love in the heart, peace of the soul, and the laughter, and not from any medicine. Health is the true wealth. Wellness is the wealth. Sleep well every night, and awake every morning replete with peace, love and the contentment. Never get angry. We all, already have, what we all need. Lead a satisfied and a healthy life. Be stable. Live in encouragement and enthusiasm. We all are one family, a big family, and the God is our only real parent. God is the parent of parents. Shift the consciousness for the positive outcomes in the life. Accept and empower the others. Never let the self-confidence to go down, of the self, and also, of other beings. Stay motivated, and be the motivator for the others. Be a healer to others for their physical pain, mental pain and the emotional pain. Instill the confidence in others. Create an environment of trust. Such an environment will then have love and respect for one another. Empowerment is the healing. Blessings are the biggest and the best accumulations, possessions, profit and the wealth of the life. Get the blessing of others. Send good energy, and the same or even better energy will be received; it is the rule and the law of the nature. Always keep good thoughts for self, and also, for the others, for everything associated with the life. Contribute in creating a better world's consciousness. Replace the word "busy" in the life, with the word "easy" in the life. Do not waste the energy, as stopping this waste of energy is creation or generation of the energy.

The quality of thoughts either wastes or preserves or conserves the energy. Mistakes and the problems are the part of the life, but the choice to respond to these, only lies with that being, and the no one else. Quieten the mind, and decide the thoughts. Confidence brings creativity. And, the creativity is connecting the seemingly unconnected. Always keep the health in good kilter. In the journey of life, with full confidence, work for a cause, and not applause. Live the life to express, and not to impress. Never strive for making the presence noticed, but behave, work and contribute in such a manner, so as to make the absence felt.

CHAPTER FORTY-FOUR

Ho'oponopono Technique

Ho'oponopono Technique practice heals all things by accepting everything. Ho'oponopono Technique teaches to take full responsibility of everything, which surrounds us. Thus, Ho'oponopono Technique encourages accountability. Ho'oponopono Technique rests on confession, repentance, and the reconciliation. Ho'oponopono Technique is an ancient Hawaiian spiritual practice. Hawaiian word "Ho'oponopono" means "to make things right". Ho'oponopono technique is a process of making things right in every relation, and the relationship with, the ancestors, the Earth, and the self. Ho'oponopono Technique eliminates negativity. Ho'oponopono technique restores the self-love. Self-love is a state of appreciation for the self. Self-love grows from the actions: actions supporting the physical, the psychological, and the spiritual growth, of the self. Self-love refers to having a high regard for self well-being, peace and the happiness. Self-love means taking care of self needs. Self-love is not sacrificing the self well-being in order to please the others. Four steps involved in the Ho'oponopono technique are, Repentance, Asking for the Forgiveness, Gratitude, and the Love. Say,

"I am sorry" for the repentance. Seek the forgiveness, whenever something goes wrong by self-action(s). Say, "Thank you" to express your gratitude. Always express your care, affection and the love. Practising the Ho'oponopono technique, heals and transforms the relations and the relationships of being with other beings, and the everything in the existence. "I'm Sorry, Please forgive me, Thank you, I Love You" is the Hopo Prayer Mantra. Hopo Prayer cleanses the practitioner of all bad feelings. Repeating the Hopo Prayer Mantra, again and again, 108 times, is a Mantra Meditation, which has magical overall positive and transforming effects on the life of its practitioner. Do not let the life remain a curate's egg.

CHAPTER FORTY-FIVE

Number 7

Number 7 is a very sacred, and also, a very spiritual number. Number 7 represents the spirituality. Number 7 has beautiful spiritual vibrations. Universe corrects us through signs and the symbols. Seeing the number 7, confirms that we are on the right path. Beings, which are associated with the number 7 are, high intellectuals, deep thinkers, philosophers, and the great scholars. Such beings analyse the things from every angle before making a correct / spot on decision. Beings associated with number 7 are visionary. Beings associated with number 7 have unique way of their thinking. Number 7 in spirituality denotes the completeness. House number totalling 7, is the abode of spiritual energies. House number totalling 7, is perfect for beings, which are looking for the spiritual growth. Number 7 helps finding the purpose and the truth of the life. A Soul Urge Number (SUN) is a number, which represents the inner characteristics of a being. Thus, if one knows the Soul Urge Number of other being, then, he or she can judge that being better before going into a relationship, or something else, which is mutual. Soul Urge Number 7 means that being has a natural affinity for seeking out knowledge and the understanding. Such a being with Soul Urge Number 7 is attracted towards the spiritual and the mystical sides of the life. A being with Soul Urge Number 7 is highly intuitive. Beings affiliated with the Number 7 are quite, insightful and wise and intellectual, truthful, and introspective. The Number 7 is a magic number. Number 7 is the number of the supreme power and the spirituality. There is a deep connection between the seven days in a week, and the planets in the Astrology. The Number 7 is associated with luck and the prosperity, and the deep matters, which influence the life. The Number 7 is an auspicious number. Music comprises of 7 notes. There are 7 wonders of the world. As per Numerology, prime numbers, 3, 7, 13, and 31 are considered to be very lucky. The Number 7 is a supernatural number. Number 7 is a number of great power. Number 7 is a number of psychic and the mystical powers. Number 7 is a number of secrecy. Beings associated with the number 7 instinctively search for the inner truth. Number 7's powers lie in the Lunar Cycle. Number 7 is mystique; it cannot be obtained by multiplying two smaller numbers together. Our first thought in morning should be "thank you". Be a "Makeba" in the life. Problems in the life are like rains, and then, being's positive attitude, acts like an umbrella, thus safeguarding him or her from its detrimental effects and negative and adverse impacts / effects. We grow in the life by learning from the mistake(s) done once. Life is a deal between the nature and the being, arranging a quid pro quo. Lucky beings get the opportunities, brilliant beings create the opportunities, and the winners use the opportunities. At times, avoiding a conflict to maintain the peace, may trigger start a war inside. Get au fait with the creation and the existence, and its designs. Panpsychism (doctrine that every material thing has an element of the consciousness) is the basis of the whole creation.

CHAPTER FORTY-SIX

Number 369

Number 369 is an Angel Number. In the Numerology, Angel Number is a number sequence of three or four numbers usually, which may be repetitive like 111 or 4444, or just the patterns like 321, 369 or 8787. Numerology is the branch of knowledge, which deals with occult significance of numbers. Angel Numbers act as a guide for deeper spiritual exploration. Angel Number sequences can range from 000 to 999. Each Angel Number has its own distinct energy, and the meaning. Angel Number is a real and very common form of the divine guidance. Angel Number 369 is a direct message from the angels that one is on the right path. Angel Number 7 signifies positive change and progress. Number 369 is associated with spiritual awakening and the enlightenment. Number 369 denotes spiritual power and transformation. Number 369 also represents the divine principles of the whole creation and the universe(s). Number 369 Manifestation Method involves writing down that thing, three times in the morning, six times in the afternoon, and nine times in the evening, which one wants to manifest in his or her life. End this Number 369 Manifestation Method with a gratitude affirmation. Sum of numbers in 360 is 9. Numbers 3, 6, and 9 are the keys to understand the universe, and the mysteries of the universe. Encountering the number 369 in the life brings all desired results in the life. Number 3 has powerful symbolism, viz. the cycle of birth-life-death, the mind-body-soul connection, the Trinity etc.. Wherever number 3 shows up in life, it's an omen of creativity, communication, optimism, and the curiosity. Number 6 refers to the strength, which we hold within ourselves. And, the number 9 helps to let go off all negativity, and the bad past. Number 369 symbolises the Law of Attraction. Number 369 creates a unique energetic resonance, which helps drawing more of what one desires into his or her experience(s). In the show and the game of the life, successful beings do, what unsuccessful beings are not willing to do; so never wish it were easier, rather, wish you were better. Only a happy being can make others happy. Never focus on the problems; problem creates more problems. Focus on the possibilities; possibility creates opportunities. For the ordinary souls, life is all about, the health, the money and the wealth, respect and the reputation, and the relationships, whereas, the life should be aimed at acquiring the wisdom, commitment, caring and its celebration. The gods are form-replication of our energies. Karma are our neurological pathways, and these neurological pathways, then create our neurological patterns, i.e. the pattern - element(s) in the memory of the subconscious mind, and thus, affect the whole life. Use your nous always. Be a spiritually awakened and enlightened distingué.

CHAPTER FORTY-SEVEN

Angel Numbers 11, 22 And 33

Angel Numbers 11, 22, and 33 are also called as the Master Numbers. In this cosmos, these super digits have a much superior presence, and contain profound energies. Mysterious forces surround these special Master Numbers. Angel Numbers 11, 22, and 33 together, make up a "Pyramid of Enlightenment", thus signifying the three stages of the whole creation, viz. envisioning, building, and the sharing. Angel Numbers 11, 22, and 33, command an extra-strength presence in the universe. Beings having Angel Numbers 11, 22, and 33 in their birth dates rise to become spiritual leaders or the community influencers. Such beings are high-decibel movers and shakers. Encountering Angel Numbers 11 or 22 or 33 in the life, is an encouraging sign of forthcoming positive changes. Appearances of these Angel Numbers, simply confirms and assures being to stay optimistic and trust his or her inner voice. These numbers are brought into our sense-perception by our Guardian Angel from time to time. Guardian Angel wants best for us. Guarding Angel uses these Angel Numbers to offer us divine guidance during tough and unpredictable times of the journey of life. Angel

Number 11 means that it is the time of the life to find the true calling. Angel Number 11 reminds of the importance of letting go of all negative connections in the life. Angel Number 11 reassures us to stay true to our intuition. Appearance of Angel Number 11 is a divine instruction to take out time from busyness of the life, and getting open and receptive to the divine guidance. Angel Number 22 is a sign of pushing forward and recognising the surrounding success. Angel Number 22 asks to keep the mind open, and expect great things to happen. Angel Number 22 asks to take action by using the personal power. Angel Number 33 tells that anything and the everything is possible. Angel Number 33 has very powerful vibrations. Angel Number 33 is associated with discipline, bravery and courage, creative thinking, deep compassion and the spiritual-level connections. Angel Number 33 resonates with the energies of honesty, blessings and the inspiration. Seeing 1122, means that angels are acknowledging our spiritual growth and awakening. Life path numbers 11 and 33 are quite compatible numbers. Numbers 11 and 33 share same energies. Angel Numbers 11 and 33 are associated with talent, and carry the potential to achieve all great things in the life. Beings having number 11 and 33, are very spiritual, and have a very strong connection to the divine. Never domineer, rather, prefer to lead the life by inspiration for others, than by intimidation. Do Yoga regularly. Do Meditation regularly inside the Pyramid.

CHAPTER FORTY-EIGHT

432 Hz. - The Divine Intelligence

432 Hz. is the divine intelligence, and the frequency of the soul. 432 Hz. is the God Note in the music. Listening to the 432 Hz. music, expands the human consciousness, by tuning into the wisdom of the universe. 432 Hz. is the frequency, at which, the universe vibrates. 432 Hz. is the frequency of the universe. Listening to a sound at 432 Hz. puts the listener in sync with the heartbeat of the Earth. 432 Hz. creates integrates the listener with the nature. 432 Hz. resonates inside the body, and thus, releases all emotional blockages. Listening to the 432 Hz. sound or tune or music, makes a being more compassionate, caring, affectionate, and the loving. 432 Hz. develops spiritual aspects of its listeners. Binaural Beats, Isochronic Tones, and the 432 Hz. music, reduce stress and anxiety. Binaural Beats are a perception of the sound, which is being created by the brain. If one listens to two tones simultaneously, both at different frequencies, with each tone in a different ear, then, the brain creates an additional tone, which is then sense-perceived, and this third tone is called as the Binaural Beat. Isochronic Tones are single tones. Isochronic Tones come on and off, like a rhythmic pulse, at regular

and evenly spaced intervals of time. Isochronic Tones are very often embedded in other sounds, like in a music, or in the sounds of the nature. Listening to a sound at 432 Hz. promotes the emotional stability. 432 Hz. gives more clarity than the 440 Hz, and thus, brings more inner peace to its listeners. Listening to 432 Hz., makes the listener calm, happy and relaxed. Listening to 432 Hz. significantly improves one's outlook of his or her life. 432 Hz. is a God-like voice. 432 Hz. music is very serene, which touches the soul in its different depths, and leads to the serendipity. 6 Hz. beat enhances all areas of the brain. 40 Hz. beat enhances responses in the frontal lobe of the brain. Frequency 528 Hz. is also known as the Solfeggio Frequency. 528 Hz. is the frequency of love. Love is one of the highest vibrating emotional states of beings. While doing Meditation, play a music, which is tuned to 432 Hz.. 432 Hz. is a miracle tone, which connects the being to his or her Spiritual Guide. In this ginormous creation, things are too mysterious, and also, quite intriguing. All knowledge and wisdom is available here only, just, one should be aware of and adept at the methods and techniques of tapping it. Picayune thinking, and the poor understanding, of the ordinary souls, about the creation, the universe, the nature, and the life, are the reasons of their failures, discontentment, wretchedness, pains, sorrows, bad health, and the miseries, in their lives.

Reiki

Word "Reiki" is a Japanese word. Reiki consists of "Rei" meaning universal, and "Ki" meaning the life energy. Word "Reiki" means "mysterious atmosphere, miraculous sign." Reiki is an energy healing technique for physical and the emotional well-being. Reiki is based on the principle of channeling healing positive energy by means of touch, and thus, Reiki activates the natural healing processes. Reiki promotes a positive mental state through gentle touch. Reiki is a meditative practice, which promotes relaxation. Reiki reduces stress and anxiety, and eliminates depression. Reiki practice is very simple and a sure and safe self-treatment. Being, who is adept at Reiki is called the Reiki Master. The Reiki Master is considered to have formally undergone a successful training in the healing art of the Reiki. During the Reiki process, the Reiki Master uses his or her very gentle hand movements with the sole intention of guiding the flow of healthy energy or the life force energy through patient or client's body. Doing so, reduces stress in the patient, and promotes his or her healing. Energy stagnates in the body in emotional pain or physical injury. Reiki releases such energy blockages within the body. Reiki Master sends a warm pulsing energy from his or her hands into the body of patient during the Reiki process. These sensations are very comforting, as Reiki energy is flowing inside the body. To practise the Reiki, close the eyes, take a few deep breaths, imagine crown of head getting opened, and a stream of healing white light entering and flowing down from top of the head, into the heart, out through the arms and the hands, and this way, activate the energy within the self. This process of Reiki practise is called the Reiki Meditation. Reiki relieves the pain in Neuropathy. Neuropathy is a nerve problem. Neuropathy may be caused by Cancer or some Cancer treatment method like Chemotherapy. Neuropathy causes weakening of muscles, numbness and tingling sensations, and swelling and pain, in different parts of the body. Usually, Neuropathy begins in the hands or the feet, and then, slowly it gets worse with the time. If a being's energy is low, then, he or she is very much likely to become unwell or get stressed. Contrary to it, if being's energy is high, then he or she is more capable of being happy and feeling well. Reiki helps the body to feel relaxed and peaceful. Reiki opens and balances the Chakras. Reiki practise allows energy to flow freely within the body, and create a balance and a harmony in the body. Reiki promotes spiritual healing, and the self-improvement. Reiki is a practice of self-care. Never be cagey about counselling. Do Yoga, Reiki Meditation, as well as have fun, become light, and celebrate the life - carpe diem, right?

CHAPTER FIFTY

Ayahuasca

Ayahuasca is a potent plant-based psychedelic. Psychedelic drugs like Lysergic Acid Diethylamide (LSD), produce hallucinations, and cause an apparent temporary expansion of the consciousness. Ayahuasca affects all senses. Ayahuasca is a psychoactive Amazonian brew. Ayahuasca is made from plants Banisteriopsis Caapi and Psychotria Viridis. There are psychoactive substances as the ingredients in the Ayahuasca. Consumption of Ayahuasca, leads to an altered level of the consciousness. Consumption of Ayahuasca, improves the insight and does the emotional healing. Also, it causes the personal growth. Ayahusca creates an experience of contact with the energies, the spirits, the deities, and the nature. Ayahuasca alters that being's, thinking, sense of the time, and the emotions, who has consumed it. Ayahuasca causes a being to powerfully hallucinate, and thus, see or hear the things, which may not exist, or are distorted. Consumption of Ayahuasca causes Near Death Experience (NDE). Ayahuasca creates contacts with the higher-dimensional beings. Ayahuasca takes the being on life-transforming voyages through the Alternative Reality. Alternative Reality refers to the parallel universes. Alternative Reality is a separate self-contained world or the universe or the reality, which coexists with this real world.

Ayahuasca decreases Neuroticism, and also, potentiates change of being's personality. Neuroticism is a trait disposition. Neuroticism relates to the experiences of various negative effects like, the self-consciousness, irritability, anger and emotional instability, and anxiety and depression. Ayahuasca is Antidepressant and Anxiolytic. Anxiolytic drugs relieve anxiety. Consumption of Ayahuasca is, purely being's decision and discretion, with all disclaimers, and, fully a matter of being's choice with absolutely no recommendations. Life is a super-duper uncharacteristic display like a wild fast-moving river, which meanders between bosky banks of, confusions, illusions, impermanence, distractions and the attractions, miseries and the happiness, failures and the success, death and the life, and the devil and the God.

CHAPTER FIFTY-ONE

Twin Flame

A Twin Flame involves two beings, which share the same soul, i.e. two halves of the same soul. When such Twin Flame meet, there is an intense magnetic attraction, strong deep connection and bonding. Twin Flame are the two souls, which meet in a lifetime. The deep residing purpose and underlying divine plan of Twin Flame is to flower their individual spirituality into its full fruition. Twin Flame may meet each other at an age of 25 $\pm$ 2 or 3 years, which is a new phase of maturity. Meeting of Twin Flame signifies a major change in the life. Twin Flame beings share a same life mission as the two embodied souls. Twin Flame relationship is a very powerful source of inspiration and motivation. Twin Flame relationship is an adventure. Twin flames reunite with one another, only after the necessary levels of their individual growth have been achieved. Twin Flame relationship urges both beings to face the challenges head-on with aplomb, and then, conquer these challenges of the life together. Twin Flame relationship has an inner soul connection. Beings in Twin Flame relationship are another's Mirror-Soul. Twin Flame may not have a romantic relationship. A Twin Flame may not necessarily be a romantic soulmate. Soulmates have a greater connection, a much deeper purpose. Twin Flame come together very energetically on a divine level. The connection of the Twin Flame is more of a higher power to enrich the other's life, whereas the soulmate connection is more concentrated on the learning and the growth of each being. Intense longing is the sign of Twin Flame's unconditional love for one another. Twin Flame can marry. The Twin Flame relationship brings up the issues, which create experience(s) and learning. Soulmate relationship is lesser intense than the Twin Flame relationship. Twin Flame relationship is much deeper and profound. Twin Flame relationship may not last longer, depending upon their karmic accumulation and design of the life. Twin Flame even get separated. Twin Flame numbers are the repeating sequence patterns. These patterns provide insight into the proximity and the depth of connection of Twin Flame journey of the togetherness. Twin Flame phenomenon occurs, when a single being of a quite high level of consciousness, gets split into two parts, and later, these two parts of same consciousness incarnate into two different physical bodies. An example could be twins, which share an energetic resemblance, rather than a biological one. In reality, Twin Flame never get separated or leave one another, as these are the two indissoluble parts of the same life force. Bond of Twin Flame is never severed or dismantled. Twin Flame bond creates the best friends. Twin Flame love can be Platonic (love, which is intimate, and also, quite affectionate, but not sexual) or simply intellectual. Mostly, it is emotionally romantic. Twin Flame journey always leads to the inner healing. In the absence of a Twin Flame partner, the other existing being, feels a stronger pull to complete the common Twin Flame's life's mission. Twin Flame can also be the soulmate, known as the "Twin-Soul", or the "Mirror-Soul", and with every high and the low of their journey of life, a better version of their love and emotions and the relationship, emerges. Twin Flame phenomenon is rare, but quite potent and powerful. Twin Flame beings receive signs about the one another. Recognition and awakening is the first stage of Twin Flame deep spiritual connection. In a given journey of the life, every being will not get into his or her Twin Flame relationship. Presence of the Twin Flame is very strongly felt. When they are near to one another, they both feel a positive charge of electricity within, with a very strong, magnetic attraction and connection. Twin Flame beings feel each other's emotions, and also, dream about one another. At times, they think about each other. After a period of separation, the Twin Flame always end up getting reunited. Twin Flame beings share similar past experiences and trauma. Beings unconscious shadow traits complicate their lives, and also, sabotage their relationships. At a certain moment, a Twin Flame being experiences some emotion, because his or her Twin Flame is also feeling same emotion at that moment. Twin Flame male and female have to finish off their respective worldly Karmas, before getting reunited in the sacred union. This sacred union of binaries, i.e. male and female Twin Flame beings, then creates a Twin Flame energy in its true rendition. Opposite polarities merge into one another, creates nullity, with nothing left. Infinity and Zero are the same points. Twin Flame phenomenon is not common. Twin flame relationships manifest only between advanced beings, which have already mastered their life lessons, and can hold the frequency of the unconditional love. Twin Flame may meet quite later in their journey of life, as it takes a lot of time and the life experiences, for them to uncover their spiritual gifts, and to share them with all. Divine Feminine (DF) wakes up first, and understands this Twin Flame connection. Twin Flame mirror each other. There is an intense latent separation sickness, till the Twin Flame do not meet each other. The Twin Flame union are quite intense and often very powerful – this includes the noticeable heart palpitations, which they both are experiencing. The Twin Flame astrological or Zodiac Signs are complementary opposite pairs like the Scorpio (Water) and the Aries (Fire), the Virgo (Earth), and the Gemini (Air), the Pisces (Water) and the Sagittarius (Fire), the Libra (Air) and the Taurus (Earth), etc.. Twin Flame are congruent at their psychological frames. Twin Flame emotions and feelings for each other are not ersatz, but all genuine. Emotions manifest either consciously or the subconsciously. Feelings are experienced consciously. We try hiding our feelings, but forget that our eyes speak out everything. Always remain filled with the joie de vivre. Be willing to "give", as in giving, we receive more. Strongest fear is, the last impression of the mind at the time of death, and we are reborn with it, in such a species, or gender, of family, time and space, so as to avenge, allay and overcome this fear. From the comfort zone, come out in the fear zone, and then, eventually reach the growth zone, through the learning zone. To grow in the life, receive animadversions quite humbly. Never be animus towards anybody or the anything. Sui generis nature of beings is their biggest gift, and the basis of the existence and the creation. Rejig the life and its format, if it is crumpled and dishevelled. A tree never bothers about the flowers, which have fallen, but remains busy making the new flowers to blossom. Similarly, life is not about what is lost, but all about what can still be sown and grown. If things are not right today, do not worry, everything will be jake again, so is the pattern and the design of the life. Through the Yoga, and the Meditation inside the Pyramid, transcendence yourself, and make yourself au fait with the greater designs of, the life, the creation, the nature and the God. It is super-duper life in the cosmos. Always value your peace more than other being's opinion about you. Past is in the head, but future is in the hands. Every being is a nonpareil, and an asset, a divine asset. Start everyday of the life with full faith and earnest prayer, and the God will give all the necessary strength to do what is just and the right, and get back that we best deserve. Blessings grace us for the entire lifetime, whereas luck stays for a moment. We all are the game. Pooh-pooh all those thoughts and the ideas, which discourage and daunt you, and bring anxiety and fear. Accept the reality. Nothing is permanent in this life. All situations and circumstances, good or bad, are pro tem. Become tolerant and forgiving. Do not be judgemental. Things which challenge us, also change us, so accept the challenges in the journey of life. Problems are the part of life, and facing them successfully, is the art of life. Every being comes a cropper, such is the design of life for all, including the gods. We suffer more in the imaginations, than in the reality. Work for a cause, a much bigger cause, and not for applause. Live the life to express, and not to impress; why to impress, you are no way better to other. We all are better and best in our ways. You are best in your way and the style, he or she is best in his or her own way and the style. God makes only one thing of its kind. No two entities are exactly same. All designs of the nature are simply, the best. Do not strive to make the presence noticed, just make the absence felt. Touch the life of others. Do good to the others, as it is a sheer joy, and also, good done always comes back in many unexpected and inexplicable ways. Be kind. Be appreciative. Smile. Stay humble. These things improve the health, and bring peace, prosperity, and the happiness. "Values" are always much important than "Valuables". You cannot please every being, but can definitely take care about hurting no one. Keep hoping for the good. If the tree inside is green, and also, blossoming, chirping trilling and singing birds will automatically come on it. Inhale the blessings. Exhale the gratitude. Quality of the life can only be raised by improving the texture of the thoughts, and deepening the depths of the understanding. What you have, every next being can have, but what you are, no other being can ever be like that, so, you and we, all are simply unique, and also the best, as created.

Growth, Progress And The Success

Growth is increasing the output in terms of certain number(s). This increase in the output is not the success. Growth is increase in one's material possessions. Growth, when added by the ethics is the Progress. Ethic means a set of moral principles, especially ones relating to the conduct. Ethic includes honesty, integrity, discipline, norms and the rules. Progress, when added by the morality, the humanity, and the spirituality, becomes the Success. Success needs pure and very high quality of thoughts. There is no end to anything in the life. Failure is never ever final, and the Success is never an end. Life is a journey with no destination. Karma, a big trap, creates the life. Life is a big illusion, a big drama, with all things temporary here, all relations are temporary, and nothing is for real, except the unconditional love. Love is the basis of everything. Love is the basis of the whole existence. Love is the God, and the God is love. Growth, Progress and the Success are always of the soul, of the energy, and never of the matter or the material. Grow within, and evolve spiritually. Spirituality is the only, true and the real, path of the life. Do Yoga, and Meditation, if possible, under the Pyramid, for their maximum benefits. Yoga and Meditation is the light, which once lit, will never get dim. The better and more you practise Yoga and the Meditation, brighter gets this flame. Growth and the Progress made, is the level achieved once for all, and are just inalienable, and are carry forwarded from being's one life to the another by him or her. We all are also immortals, like the 7 immortals, viz. the Ashwatthama, the Bali, the Vyasa, the Hanuman, the Vibhishana, the Kripacharya and the Parashurama, as our essence, i.e. the true self or the real self, never dies. The path undertaken for the journey of life is not a cul-de-sac, but the path infinite continuum, a continuous journey. This book, and other books by the author, viz. Life, Death - demystified, Himalaya - The Spiritual Abode, Experiencing the God, Tere Bina - without you, the Ghost, Power of Subconscious Mind, becoming Rich - True Richness, Power of Positive Thinking, beyond the BLOOD - my biggest family and The Secret of Happiness, of spirituality, i.e. the Life Engineering books, by this author are, a great healer of its times, the best-sellers, and a complete guide for leading a good meaningful life - not an apocrypha, but an anthology of Dr. Yaduvir Singh canon.

The Path Of Spirituality And The Books On Life Engineering

The path of the Spirituality is the only real path of the life, which leads to the peace, joy and the happiness, in the life. It gives the life, a meaning, a greater purpose, a right direction and the bid success. Spirituality brings the fulfillment in the life. Spirituality and its practices, are the only guide for the life. Spirituality is the path to experience the universe, and also, the God. Understand the spirituality, and the life. A sincere reading of this book, "Pyramid", which deals with the Pyramids, the Meditation, and the other related aspects, is highly recommended to all living on the planet in the present times, as it will bring the desired changes in their life. This book, "Pyramid", if read sincerely, and also, understood, will bring peace, joy, happiness, and the satisfaction, in the life. Other best-sellers (books) on Life Engineering (Spirituality) genre by the same Author are, "The Secret of Happiness", "Beyond the Blood, "Power of Positive Thinking", "Becoming Rich", "Power of Subconscious Mind", "The Ghost", "Tere Bina - Without You", "Experiencing the God", "Himalaya - The Spiritual Abode", "Death - Demystified", and "Life - A Continuous Journey". Another interesting book, by the same author, falling into a different genre is "2020 & 2021 - The Cartoon Book".

9 798891 330764